Money and Macro Policy

Recent Economic Thought Series

Warren J. Samuels, Editor
Michigan State University
East Lansing, Michigan, U.S.A.

Other titles in the series:

Feiwel, G.R., *Samuelson and Neoclassical Economics*

Wade, L.L., *Politial Economy: Modern Views*

Zimbalist, A., *Comparative Economic Systems: Recent Views*

Darity, W., *Labor Economics: Modern Views*

This series is devoted to works that present divergent views on the development, prospects, and tensions within some important research areas of international economic thought. Among the fields covered are macromonetary policy public finance labor and political economy. The emphasis of the series is on providing a critical, constructive view of each of these fields, as well as a forum through which leading scholars of international reputation may voice their perspectives on important related issues. Each volume in the series will be self-contained, together these volumes will provide dramatic evidence of the variety of economic thought within the scholarly community.

Money and Macro Policy

Marc Jarsulic
Editor

Kluwer-Nijhoff Publishing
a member of the Kluwer Academic Publishers Group
Boston-Dordrecht-Lancaster

Contents

Contributing Authors

Alfred S. Eichner, Department of Economics, Rutgers University

Leonard Forman, Chief Economist, *The New York Times*

Miles Groves, Economic Analyst, *The New York Times*

Joseph Halevi, Department of Economics, University of Sydney, Australia

Marc Jarsulic, Department of Economics, Vassar College

Jane Knodell, Department of Economics, University of Denver

Marc Lavoie, Department of Economics, University of Ottawa, Canada

David Levine, Department of Economics, University of Denver

Basil Moore, Department of Economics, Wesleyan University

Stephen Rousseas, Department of Economics, Vassar College

Juliet B. Schor, Department of Economics, Harvard University

Distributors for North America:

Kluwer Academic Publishers
190 Old Derby Street
Hingham, MA 02043, U.S.A.

Distributors outside North America:

Kluwer Academic Publishers Group
Distribution Centre
P.O. Box 322
3300AH Dordrecht
The Netherlands

Library of Congress Cataloging in Publication Data
Main entry under title:

Money and macro policy.

(Recent economic thought series)
Bibliography: p.
Includes index.
1. Money—Addresses, essays, lectures. 2. Macro-economics—Addresses, essays, lectures. 3. Economic policy—Addresses, essays, lectures. I. Jarsulic, Marc. II. Series: Recent economic thought.
HG221.M8159 1984 339.5′3 84-9743
ISBN 0-89838-127-4

Preface

In recent years Monetarist theory and its policy prescriptions have had significant impact on the economics profession and on economic policy. Graduate courses and undergraduate textbooks give serious attention to models which take full-employment Walrasian equilibrium as a good description of the center of gravity of market economies, then graft on an exogenous money stock to account for price inflation and business cycles. Monetary authorities in the United States and United Kingdom have adopted restrictive monetary policies, ostensibly to deal with inflation, with very large consequences for output and employment. To their credit, many economists who have an utterly orthodox attachment to Walrasian ideas do not think much of Monetarism. James Tobin, in *Asset Accumulation and Economic Activity*, takes current Monetarist thinking to task in many ways, but especially for *assuming* that markets always clear. Frank Hahn, in *Money and Inflation*, faults Monetarists for not integrating money into the Walrasian model before drawing conclusions about the effects of money on equilibrium. However, the critical responses of these and other eminent economists seem to make very little headway. It is likely that this failure comes in part because their theoretical perspective is so close to that of their adversaries. The disputes seem to be over how literally to take the shared paradigm of general equilibrium.

The essays in this book offer very different views of money and macroeconomics. The first four essays concern aspects of the emerging Post Keynesian approach to money. The essay by Moore and the essay by Forman, Groves, and Eichner discuss the theoretical framework and some empirical evidence supporting the view that the money supply is endogenously determined. The essay by Rousseas focuses on some interesting early recognition of the importance of financial innovations in determining the supply of money and credit. In his contribution, Lavoie surveys the Post Keynesian position and compares it to the overdraft and dynamic circuit approaches.

The four remaining essays show a concern for relating monetary questions to classical and neo-Marxian theory. Halevi analyzes the ideas of Baran and Sweezy and discusses the importance of finance to their framework. Knodell and Levine use the concepts of industrial and financial circulations to argue that economic crisis is financial in origin and that attempts to limit crisis generate significant social contradictions. Schor develops evidence on wage and price flexibility, which suggests that restrictive monetary policy may be tied to problems of profitability. In the final essay, I suggest that Keynes' analysis of effective demand, adopted without Marxian insights about production and distribution, offers an inadequate alternative to Monetarist ideas.

While the approaches taken in this volume are diverse, the contributions have at least two things in common: they take macroeconomics seriously, and they attempt to offer fresh insights into the role of money. Overall this makes for stimulating reading and is suggestive of new and interesting lines of inquiry.

M.J.

1 WAGES, BANK LENDING, AND THE ENDOGENEITY OF CREDIT MONEY

Basil Moore

Monetary theory is less abstract than most economic theory; it cannot avoid a relation to reality, which in other economic theory is sometimes missing.

—Sir John Hicks, *Critical Essays in Monetary Theory*.

1. Introduction

The traditional view of the bank money-creation process relies on the bank reserves-deposits relation. Central banks are posited to be able to control the quantity of bank deposits, and thereby the money stock, by determining the size of the high-powered base. Since commercial banks have an incentive to economize on holdings of excess reserves, the long-run ratio of bank reserves to deposits ordinarily is fairly stable. As a result it is a simple matter to determine the deposit-reserve multiplier. The argument seems both plausible and convincing. Introductory students of economics are taught how central banks, through open-market operations, affect increases or decreases in bank reserves to control the quantity of bank deposits. But its apparent simplicity should perhaps really make one suspicious. If it is so easy for central banks to control the rate of growth of monetary aggregates by controlling the supply of bank reserves, how do we explain the recent failure of monetary targeting throughout the entire western world?

Because they have been unable to specify the transmission mechanism by which monetary change appears empirically to spill over so rapidly into product and factor markets, Monetarists have repeatedly been accused of having a "Black Box" in their models. Post-Keynesians argue that it is money-wage growth which is more nearly exogenous, which central banks validate by adjusting the money stock. But until they are able to specify more precisely the mechanism by which changes in money wages influence the money supply, post-Keynesians are similarly open to the accusation of having a "Black Box." Why in fact are central banks observed to accommodate? Lack of moral fibre is surely not a sufficient explanation.

2. The Quantity Theory: A Historical Review

The essence of Monetarism is that the rate of increase of the money stock is the primary determinant of the rate of increase of nominal income (Laidler, 1981; Tobin, 1981). Inflation is held to be caused primarily by a rate of increase of the money stock in excess of that warranted by the rate of growth of real output. In the long run, the behavior of the real economy is regarded as largely neutral to monetary disturbances and fully determined by real factors, primarily the rate of growth of the supply of labor and capital, and the rate of technical progress. This leads to the monetarists' main policy recommendation: *a lower rate of growth of the nominal money-stock is a necessary and sufficient condition for reducing the rate of inflation over the longer term.*

Implicit in this position is the assumption that money has an exogenous supply schedule, so that the quantity available is determined independently of the demand for it, and can, in principle at least, be controlled by the central bank (Kaldor, 1982). Monetarists do not recognize the distinction between demand-inflation and cost-inflation. They argue that wages and other costs are derived from prices, and prices rise due to excess demand in some or all markets as a result of an excess supply of money balances. Central banks are assumed to set the *nominal* amount of money balances. But the *real* amount of money balances demanded is determined by the public's (stable) demand for money function (Friedman and Schwartz, 1982, Ch. 2). This has somewhat derisively been termed the "Hot Potato" Theory of Money (Tobin, 1981). Prices rise as individual households and firms attempt to get rid of (spend) their excess nominal money balances. But for the economy as a whole, the aggregate nominal money stock is exogenously given, as determined by the central bank. Inflation will continue until prices have risen sufficiently to reduce the real value of money balances to their desired level, so that the excess supply of money has been eliminated.

Modern Monetarism derives directly from the Quantity Theory of Money, which dominated both economic and political thought in the nineteenth and early twentieth century. The Quantity Theory asserted that the value of money, like any other good, varies in inverse proportion to its quantity. This relationship was expressed in two alternate forms:

$$MV = py = Y \tag{1.1}$$

$$M = kpy = kY \tag{1.2}$$

In the first, the Fisher form, velocity (V) expresses the number of times that a unit of money circulates as income each year. In the second, the Cambridge form, k denotes the demand to hold wealth in the form of money expressed as some proportion of annual income.

Marshall and Walras believed that the nominal value of money balances (M) was given exogenously by the quantity of gold in existence. The mechanism that brought nominal balances into conformity with desired real balances was changes in the value of gold in relation to other commodities. The existence of paper money presented an obvious complication for this doctrine. But it was concluded that, provided the banking system worked under rules which maintain a fixed relation between the supply of bank money and an external base, it was still possible to argue that the nominal quantity of fiat paper money in circulation was determined exogenously by the monetary authorities. It was not, after all, the intrinsic value of gold which determined its value, but rather its limited quantity in relation to the demand for it (Hicks, 1977, pp. 50–61).

This was the dominant doctrine on which all Anglo-Saxon economists were brought up. Its implications were that inflation is always the result of an overissue of bank notes (to use Ricardo's original expression), whether caused by the financial needs of governments, as in times of war, or the latitude of central banks in permitting the Banking System to extend too much credit.

Keynes' intellectual development may be viewed as a long struggle to escape from this theory. He succeeded in doing so imperfectly, and only in stages. The first stage was the realization that the labor market is different from commodity markets, in that wages do not adjust automatically to changes in demand so as to eliminate an excess supply of labor. Hence his opposition to the return to the Gold Standard at prewar parity after World War I. Keynes held that the domestic price level was tied to the level of domestic wages, which do not readily adjust downward so as to keep supply and demand in equilibrium.

The second stage came with his realization that effective aggregate demand for commodities is determined not by monetary factors but by autonomous investment and government expenditures, combined with the multiplier, which depended on the stable propensity to save out of income. This meant that saving and investment were brought into equality *ex post* through the adjustment of the level of nominal income, and not, as the traditional theory had it, through movements in the rate of interest. This left the rate of interest "in the air," as Keynes himself put it, until he developed the idea of liquidity preference.

This solution represented a *modification* of the Quantity Theory, but not its *abandonment*. Keynes wrote $=L(Y, r)$ or $M=k(r)Y$, where $L(Y, r)$ represents the demand for money as a function of both the level of income and the interest rate, while $k(r)$ represents the demand for money expressed as a proportion of income, which is inversely related to the rate of interest. The demand for money will be greater the lower the rate of interest, so that it was the money market and not saving and investment which was equilibrated through interest-rate adjustment.

Keynes' formulation seemed to imply, both to him and to others, that all the adjustments of monetary to autonomous demand factors came through changes in the velocity of circulation. It was this which led economists in the immediate postwar period to downplay the importance of monetary policy. Perhaps the best illustration of this phase is the now extreme-sounding statements of the Radcliffe committee about the variability of velocity:

> "We cannot find any reason for supporting, or any experience in monetary history indicating that there is any limit to the velocity of circulation; it is a statistical concept that tells us nothing directly of the motivation that influences the level of total demand" (Radcliffe, 1959, Para. 391).

This formulation also persuaded Friedman that the empirical validity of the Keynesian theory depended on the *absence* of any close correlation between M and Y. If variations in Y result primarily in adjustments of V, then Y and M should not be closely correlated. Friedman's emphatic reassertion of the Quantity Theory of Money was based essentially on the close empirical correlation he found to exist between income and variously defined monetary aggregates, a relationship he found, to the profession's astonishment, more stable than Keynes' multiplier (Friedman and Meiselman, 1963). Friedman interpreted this empirical stability of velocity as implying the existence of a stable demand function for money (Friedman and Schwartz, 1982, Ch. 2).[1]

There is nothing necessarily inconsistent between Monetarist reasoning and scenarios in which wage or import price increases induce the monetary authorities to expand the money stock, in order to avoid the short-term increases in unemployment which would otherwise result. But these issues concerning the behavior of the monetary authorities, while logically quite separate from the disputes between monetarists and Keynesians about the behavior of the private sector in response to variations in monetary variables, do have a direct bearing on the interpretation of the empirical evidence for the monetarist explanation of a primarily one-way causal relationship between monetary growth and price inflation.

Monetarists have demonstrated that changes in nominal income are systematically associated with changes in the money stock. This relationship has been shown to hold for many countries over many periods. But a fairly close long-term statistical association is one thing; the direction of the causal influence implicit in this correlation is another. Monetarists are of course aware of the two-way relationship between money and money income.

> "Changes in the money stock are therefore a consequence as well as an independent source of change in money income and prices, though, once they occur, they produce still further effects on income and prices. Mutual interaction but with money rather the senior partner in longer-run movements and in major cyclical movements, and more nearly an equal partner with money income and prices in shorter-run and milder movements—this is the generalization suggested by our evidence" (Friedman and Schwartz, 1963, p. 695).

Their case for the exogeneity of monetary change rests primarily on the fact that the money stock is ultimately under the direct control of the central bank.[2]

When money is metallic money, its supply can be treated as an exogenous variable. Major changes in supply come in from outside, for example with new gold discoveries. David Hume, in his *Essay on Money*, used as his historical example the influx of gold and silver from the Spanish possessions in America between 1550 and 1600 to explain the rise in the price level in Spain and then Europe during the same period.[3] There is no question in such a case that the supply of money is exogenous. Hume was aware that the initial effect of an increase in the supply of money was to stimulate industry: "It must first quicken the diligence of every individual before it increase the price of labour" (Hume, 1955). A possible effect on output as well as on prices must, therefore, be allowed for. But whatever its effects, there can be no doubt that the influx of silver was in a meaningful sense the *cause* of the increase in the nominal value of total output.

The use of banking builds upon the base of metallic money a pyramid of money substitutes, which gradually become firmer, until finally the transfer of a banker's promise to pay is regarded as closing a transaction. At the end of the nineteenth century, the primarily metallic money (gold) was still in general use, even though a substantial superstructure of bank credit had been built upon it. The national currencies of individual countries were kept convertible, at approximately fixed parities, into the money metal. Initially, economists insisted on regarding only the gold base as *the* money; the rest being money substitutes, which enable the gold base to support a larger value of output. Looked at this way, the Quantity Theory does not need to be greatly changed. There is still an equilibrium path of output, determined by the supply of gold. The possibilities of fluctuation would simply be larger, as the available gold would be sometimes more fully and sometimes less fully used. But the independence of the gold base would serve to keep the fluctuations within limits.

Nevertheless gold was even then already passing out of private circulation. It was becoming a specialized money, used by banks in settling accounts with one another, in particular for international transactions, but much less used outside the banking system. Gradually economists came to regard bank money as *the* money. If the Quantity Theory was to be maintained, it was to the quantity of bank or credit money that it must apply. This step was generally taken, and by modern Monetarists is still taken. Nevertheless it is a serious step, which makes a very considerable difference to the argument (Hicks, 1977).

There is no question that when money is metallic money, its supply can be treated as an exogenous variable. But the supply of bank money is not so clearly exogenous. It can, it is true, be affected by changes in central banking policy. But with any given policy, as represented for example by the level of central-bank lending rates, the supply of bank money is more or less completely determined by market forces governing bank assets. Deposits are created by the banks whenever they add to their assets and grant additional loans. In both retail credit and deposit markets, banks operate as price-setters and quantity-takers. As a result the volume of bank intermediation in nominal terms is largely determined by the demand for bank credit. Bank credit is provided by the banks on demand, to the extent the market requires, and so is *not* an exogenous variable (Kaldor, 1982).

In practice, however, this endogeneity of the money stock has been concealed, because the banking system works under rules imposed upon it which maintain a fixed attachment between the supply of bank money and an external base (in the Gold Standard period, the supply of gold). These rules are apparently inflexible, so that the supply of bank money *appears* to be a direct function of the monetary base. Since this consists of the liabilities of the central bank, it seems to follow that the money supply can be regarded as an exogenous variable. This interpretation is consistent with most contemporary descriptions of the working of the monetary system (fiduciary issues, reserve requirements, deposit multipliers, etc.) in which the quantity of money appears mechanically determined by the high-powered base.[4] The significant point, however, is that the high-powered base is no longer rigidly tied to any external gold-stock. Central banks have the freedom to vary the base so as to make it consistent with any nominal volume of bank intermediation. In economies where credit money is *the* money, it is *banking policy*, rather than the *stock of money*, which becomes the exogenous variable.

This was originally developed by Wicksell, in his model of a pure credit economy. All money is simply someone's promise to pay. If there is in fact no *hard* metallic money in which payment can be made, all that can be promised is the convertibility of one promise into another promise, which the creditor may at the moment prefer. When there is one agent the reliability of whose promises is always greater than the reliability of any other's (in the case of national economies the central bank, whose liabilities alone can be legal tender) the other's promises to pay are superseded. In the international economy, where there is no central bank and so no legal tender, this does not occur. Wicksell in effect postulated that there exist a group of institutions whose promises to pay have maximum reliability. The promise to pay by each is a promise to exchange its promise, if required to do so, into a promise issued by another.

Such a group of institutions, by maintaining this relationship, may be regarded as a Banking System issuing pure credit money. The funds which they lend are funds which they have borrowed. In order to extend its business, any individual bank must seek to borrow more in order to have more to lend. Individual banks are in competition with one another. In seeking to attract funds, a bank must pay interest and/or provide non-pecuniary services on its deposits, the funds that it borrows. A bank's lending rate will have to exceed its borrowing rate, so as to cover its costs and make a profit. However in a competitive system this margin will be quite stable and narrow.

In constructing a simple model of a pure credit system, it seems appropriate to neglect the margin between lending and borrowing rates. This margin will be relatively constant, as determined by the technological efficiency and competitive structure of the Banking System. Wicksell let this pair of interest rates be represented by a single rate of interest, which becomes the effective monetary regulator. A rise in lending rates deters borrowing, and a rise in deposit rates deters spending, and conversely. As a result reductions in *the* interest rate are expansionary, increases in *the* interest rate contractionary. The fact that historical evidence reveals that rates of interest were usually high when prices were rising, and low when they were falling, simply implies that, on the whole, the Banking System was acting as a stabilizer. *Ceteris paribus*, expansion would be greater (or contraction less) at lower rates of interest than higher. Rising prices in a boom increased the demand for loans, while falling prices in a slump diminished loan demand.[5]

Wicksell distinguished sharply between trend and cycle. In Keynes this distinction had disappeared. That is why in the *General Theory* he threw over Wicksell's natural rate, of which in the *Treatise* he had approved. He did so because he threw over Wicksell's long-term equilibrium, an equilibrium trend which left room for cyclical fluctuations about it. In Wicksell's equilibrium there is normal employment. To Keynes, writing in the Great Depression with the decade of the twenties behind him, normal employment seemed uninteresting. Full employment, the maximum employment that can be attained by expansion of effective demand, was the only benchmark that appeared relevant. Long-term equilibrium having disappeared, the way was clear for concentration on the economics of the short period. So Keynes's equilibrium is quite different from Wicksell's. It is just the state in which short-term demand forces have had time to work themselves out.

In Keynes's system there is a developed financial system. As a result it should be nearer the Wicksell model than the Quantity Theory. Nevertheless in the *General Theory* Keynes treats the supply of money, which is taken to be credit money, as exogenous. In order to reconcile his income-expenditure determination of the level of money income with the Quantity Theory explanation, Keynes took the route of stressing the variability of velocity. Thus when Friedman was able to show the rough longer-run stability of velocity, irrespective of the monetary aggregate used, the Keynesian system appeared severely threatened.[6]

Unlike the *Treatise*, the *General Theory* devotes very little analysis to the Banking System ("technical monetary details fall in the background"). While it is true that lending rates had fallen to low levels in the Depression, they were still sufficiently positive to be above the required margin of banking intermediaries, so that competition still maintained positive, albeit low, deposit rates. Keynes proceeded as if the return on deposits were zero, which led to his famous inquiry of why anyone would wish to hold such an asset? *The* interest rate for Keynes was the rate on long-term bonds. Keynes was wrong in not following Wicksell and relating this to the return paid on deposits, especially since he did not want to rely on the assumption of monopolistic market structures for his results.[7]

One important consequence of credit money is that, unlike a metallic money system, it is no longer appropriate to assume that funds are unlikely to be borrowed unless it is intended that they should immediately be spent. For to borrow from and then redeposit with the Banking System now involves only a small sacrifice of interest, the spread between bank borrowing and lending rates. The additional liquidity gained may be worth the price. A much more important consequence is that, in all sophisticated financial systems, borrowers enter into formal agreements with their banks for a prearranged line of credit. For a modest fee the additional liquidity gained by such unutilized credit commitments is clearly desirable. Credit and money then both become demand-determined.

It is these two facts, more than anything else, which make the Quantity Theory inapplicable to a credit-money economy. A substantial part of the total quantity of credit money may at times be held idle, so that the link between the total quantity of money and the part of it which circulates is snapped. This is Keynes's position, suggesting a potentially greater variability in the income velocity of money. More important but less recognized, even by Keynes, changes in the total quantity of money are determined primarily by changes in the demand for bank credit. The quantity of bank loans becomes demand-determined, as does the quantity of bank deposits. As a result the quantity of credit money is endogenously determined by market forces.

3. The Bank Money-Creation Process

The traditional view of the bank money creation process relies on the bank reserves-multiplier relation ($M = mB$) (Cagan, 1965). The central bank is posited to be able to affect the quantity of bank deposits, and thereby the money stock, by determining the nominal amount of the high-powered reserve base (B). The value of the reserve multiplier (m) is determined by the public's currency-deposit ratio and the bank's cash reserve ratio. It can be shown that, except in the very short-run, the money multiplier is fairly stable, so that most of the change in the money stock is attributable to changes in the monetary base. Since the base is the liability of the central bank, and so is affected by central bank purchases or sales of financial assets, Monetarists hold that the money stock is ultimately under the control of the central bank, and therefore is properly considered an exogenous variable.

The conventional view is correct that the nominal volume of bank intermediation is determined by the volume of bank assets. But it fails to recognize the distinction between marketable and nonmarketable assets in bank portfolios. By proceeding as if changes in the high-powered base *originate* in the act of central bank purchase or sale of securities (open market operations), to which commercial banks respond by buying or selling assets so as to eliminate reserve excesses or deficiencies, the analysis implicitly proceeds as if commercial banks were able to adjust their portfolios, upwards or downwards, entirely at their own initiative. This would be accurate *only* if commercial bank assets were in fact held primarily in marketable securities: government or corporate bonds.

The conventional view correctly applies to initiatives on the part of the central bank to *increase* the money stock. By providing the commercial banks with excess reserves through open-market purchases, banks always have the opportunity to increase their asset portfolios by purchasing additional marketable securities. They will in general prefer to hold securities rather than zero interest-bearing excess reserves, so long as the yield on securities is positive. The only exception is when the return on short-term securities has been driven to a very low level, for example a fraction of one percent, as occurred in the United States in the late 1930s. At such yields the banks may chose voluntarily to hold substantial excess reserves, since the opportunity cost of holding excess reserves is then very low. Very large branch banks, recognizing that such yields are below their marginal cost of raising additional deposit funds, might be aware that to the extent they have any positive net deposit inflow as a result of larger security holdings (a credit-deposit multiplier in excess of zero), such security purchases might actually lower their net profits. But in general the central bank ordinarily has the power to *increase* the money stock exogenously at its discretion.

But because it does not distinguish marketable and nonmarketable securities, the conventional account fails to recognize an important asymmetry. The central bank, while it can always *increase* the money stock exogenously, may be unable to initiate exogenous *decreases* in the money stock. If the commercial banks held their assets primarily in marketable securities, this asymmetry would not occur. The central bank would be able to initiate decreases as easily as increases in the money stock. In response to a reserve deficiency, commercial banks would then be able simply to reduce their asset portfolios by selling marketable securities until their required reserve ratios had been restored, as in the conventional explanation.

However the raison d'être of commercial banks is to make short-term loans to finance the legitimate credit needs of their customers, primarily industrial and commercial companies. Such loans differ from securities in two important respects. First they are nonmarketable. Banks and borrowers both cultivate an important customer relationship. Due to the fact that the credit position of the borrower is in general known only to the lending bank, to the outside public such IOUs will be perceived as heterogeneous with regard to risk. As a result, like all heterogeneous assets, no well-developed secondary market exists on which they can be bought and sold. Thus, in spite of their typical short maturity, bank loans are illiquid to the lending bank. They cannot be turned quickly, cheaply, and conveniently into cash. Once granted, they cannot be reduced until they mature.

The second differentiating characteristic of bank loans is that they are typically made *at the initiative of the borrower*, not the lender. While bankers may attempt to sell credit by various loan promotion schemes, in general the initiative to take out, renew, or increase a loan always rests with the borrower. Commercial bank loan officers attempt to ensure that loan requests meet their bank's income and asset collateral requirements, and satisfy themselves concerning the validity of the project and the credit standing and character of the borrower. It is for this reason that banks and borrowers develop client relationships. Commercial banks have a strong competitive incentive to attempt to meet all legitimate, reasonable loan requests from their regular customers. Virtually all large companies in the United States have prearranged lines of credit facilities with several banks. In the United Kingdom, banks rely overwhelmingly on previously negotiated overdraft limits.[8] Banks set the lending rate charged, and attempt to meet all the resulting loan demand that satisfies their minimum collateral risk standards. The quantity of loans granted under such circumstances is virtually completely demand-determined. Banks ordinarily cannot increase or reduce their loan portfolios at their initiative.

The ability of central banks to effectuate an exogenous reduction in the money stock will thus depend critically on the composition of bank portfolios. It will vary with the period considered and the strength of the underlying demand for bank loans. In periods when bank asset portfolios include a large proportion of marketable government or corporate securities, as was the case during the Depression of the 1930s and during the immediate postwar boom period, central banks will be able to initiate exogenous reductions in bank-asset portfolios by open-market sales of securities. Moreover, even in periods when the demand for bank credit is increasing rapidly, such as the immediate postwar period, while the central bank may be unable to restrict the rate of expansion of bank-loan portfolios, it will be able to restrict the overall rate of expansion of bank total assets by reserve management, by forcing the banks to sell marketable securities to finance their loan additions.

However by the late 1960s, banks in both the United States and the United Kingdom had reduced their government security holdings towards the minimum levels required for secondary reserve liquidity needs, as bank loans had been restored to their original primacy position in bank-asset portfolios.

In the United States, in response to the first credit crunch instigated by the Federal Reserve's reluctance to provide bank liquidity on demand in the 1960's, banks increasingly adopted liability management, or what is sometimes termed liability-side liquidity. In order to assure that they will have the funds to meet additional loan requests, banks took the initiative of selling negotiable certificates of deposit (CDs) both at home and, as importantly, abroad in the Eurodollar market. This development was followed by banks in the United Kingdom. The pace of expansion of the volume of bank intermediation has thus been increasingly governed by the rate of expansion of bank-loan portfolios, which in turn is largely determined by changes in the demand for bank credit.

As a result, in response to a credit-driven increase in the money supply, powered primarily by increases in the demand for bank loans, the monetary authorities are rendered relatively impotent in their ability to restrict the rate of growth of the money stock. Once banks have acquiesced to an increased demand for credit, and their asset portfolios and total deposits have expanded proportionately, it becomes nearly impossible for the central bank to restrict directly the growth of any chosen monetary aggregate, other than by raising short-term interest rates and inducing economic units to reallocate their asset portfolios.

Since bank loans are not marketable, once granted they cannot be resold so as to reduce the size of bank-asset portfolios. Moreover while nominally short term, many bank loans are typically rolled over and renewed when they mature. All the banks can do, individually or collectively, is restrict the rate at which they accede to new loan requests. But since, as stated, bank loan commitments already outstanding are characteristically about double the volume of loans actually granted, banks themselves have very little ability to reduce the rate of loan expansion, at least to their regular customers who make up the bulk of bank borrowing. Once banks have reduced their portfolios of marketable securities towards the minimum secondary reserve levels required for liquidity purposes, as necessary to maintain their instant repurchase clause on their deposit liabilities, the central bank has no choice but to make the required reserves available on demand to support the larger volume of bank intermediation, i.e, to accommodate the increased demand for bank credit. The central bank does always retain the power to set the interest rate at which it will provide such lender of last resort liquidity reserves; but it has little or no ability to constrain the amount of reserves provided quantitatively below the demand for them. Moreover, in open economies central banks will be constrained by foreign-exchange reserve and exchange-rate considerations from setting domestic interest rates too far out of line with the levels ruling in foreign financial centers.

4. A Simple Model of the Banking Firm

The growth of nominal bank deposits, and so the behavior of the nominal money stock, is determined as shown above by the growth of bank assets. Whenever banks purchase assets, deposits are created in the process. Increases in the supply of individual deposits will always be accepted by wealthowners for transactions purposes, so long as deposits retain their general acceptability as means of payments. The quantity of deposits, like the quantity of loans, is always demand-determined, since banks administer the interest rate offered and accept whatever quantity are demanded. At the same time the quantity of nominal deposits demanded will be governed by the quantity of nominal deposits supplied by the banks in the process of adding to their asset portfolios.

Banks may be considered as two-input, two-output firms (Wills, 1982). The two inputs (bank liabilities) are retail and wholesale deposits; the two outputs (bank assets) are retail and wholesale lending. Total bank lending and total bank deposits are linked through the balance-sheet identity. Individual banks are price-setters and quantity-takers in both their retail deposit and loan markets.

Banks must attempt to satisfy simultaneously both the demand for loans and the demand for deposits. But bank borrowers and bank depositers are different economic units. There is nothing to assure that, for any individual bank or for the system as a whole, the quantity of loans demanded will automatically equal the quantity of deposits demanded. Banks make loans and accept deposits on demand, providing as stated that loan requests meet their minimum collateral and risk requirements. They must then meet any net surplus or deficit of funds in the wholesale markets, which are the source of or repository for banks' excess funds.

The ebb and flow of funds to the wholesale market produce fluctuations in wholesale interest rates. Wholesale instruments are typically marketable, so that such assets and liabilities are highly liquid. Individual banks will set their administered retail loan and deposit rates with reference to their marginal cost of funds in the wholesale market. As a result, cumulative changes in market-determined wholesale rates will be reflected with a lag in changes in administered retail rates.

In the short run the adjustment of administered retail loan and deposit rates will not be sufficient to equate the demand for loans and deposits. The buffer needed to absorb these short-term differences is provided by the wholesale markets and ultimately by the central bank. So long as the central bank is prepared to provide extra short-term funds to the banking system at close to ruling rates, the banks do not need to maintain large secondary liquidity

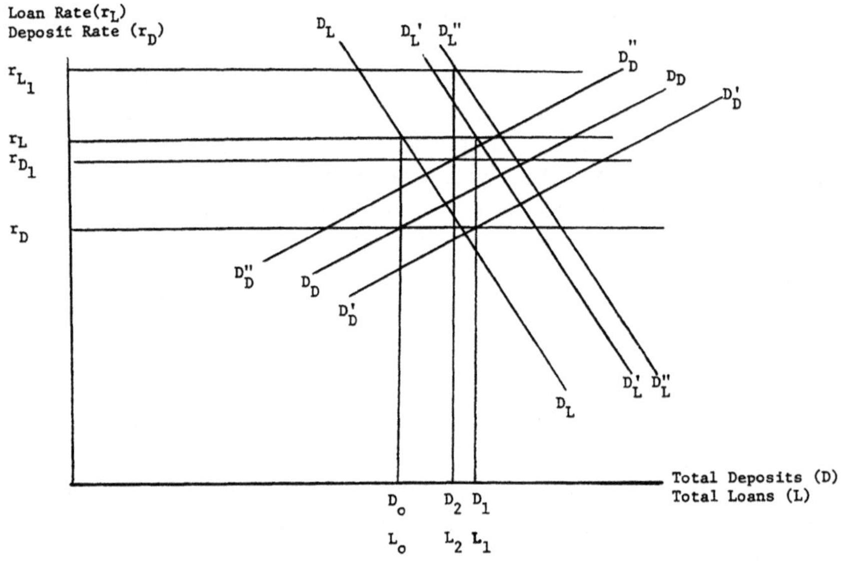

Figure 1-1

reserves. Over the longer term the banks must adjust their administered deposit and lending rates until the quantity of loans and the quantity of deposits demanded is brought into the banks' desired loan/deposit balance-sheet position.

The situation is shown diagrammatically in figure 1-1. For simplicity bank reserves and net worth are omitted. In the initial equilibrium position ($D_o = L_o$) the demand for bank loans is represented by D_LD_L, and the demand for bank deposits by D_DD_D. The difference between loan and deposit rates ($r_L - r_D$) represents the normal profit spread. An increase in loan demand, e.g., to $D_L'D_L'$, will result in an equal increase in banks loans and deposits ($D_1 = L_1$), so long as all the additional deposits created are re-lent by depositors to the Banking System.

It is in this sense that the volume of nominal lending *by* the Banking System determines the volume of nominal lending *to* the Banking System. In the long run the situation is reversed. The volume of real lending by the Banking System is determined by the volume of real deposits that the banks are able to attract.

If, in response to an autonomous increase in loan demand, the central bank choses to raise the rate at which it is willing to supply reserves, wholesale rates will rise. The result will be to cause a further increase in the demand for bank loans, e.g., to $D_L''D_L''$, and to reduce the demand for bank deposits, e.g., to $D_D''D_D''$. In the new equilibrium, administered lending and deposit rates will rise until the quantity of loans and deposits demanded is equated ($D_2 = L_2$), and the original profit spread has been restored ($r_L - r_D = r_{L_1} - r_{D_1}$).

The above analysis makes explicit the fact that the banks' supply of loans and deposits functions are always horizontal, whatever the interest rate. It follows that the quantity of loans and deposits is always demand-determined. So long as there exist alternative liquid-assets, there *can* never be excess supply or demand for nominal deposits. Economic units always have the opportunity to eliminate an excess supply of nominal deposits by purchasing liquid assets or by reducing their outstanding loans. Similarly they can always eliminate an excess demand for nominal deposits by increasing their bank borrowing, or reducing their liquid-asset portfolios.

5. Endogenous Money Stock: Reverse Causality

It follows that the direction of causality implicit in both the reserves-deposit relation and the money-income relation is precisely the opposite of that held by the conventional view. The traditional characterization of the money-supply process, which views changes in some exogenously controlled reserve base as causing changes in some monetary aggregate, is fundamentally incorrect. To the extent there is a stable relationship between the high-powered base and the money stock, and between the money stock and aggregate money income, the causal relationship implied is more like the reverse of the traditional view. The evidence suggests that the quantity of bank deposits over the longer run is determined primarily by the demand for bank credit. "In the real world banks extend credit, creating deposits in the process, and look for the reserves later" (Holmes, 1969, p. 73). Whenever the increase in the money stock is a by-product of increased borrowing from the banking system, whether by the public or the private sector, the increase in the supply of money is a *consequence* of increased loan expenditure, not the *cause* of it, which the central bank can influence only indirectly by changing short-term interest rates. Both the high-powered base and the money stock are then in fact endogenous.

The empirical evidence supporting the view that the money stock is endogenous and not really a control variable is of at least four sorts. First this is what central bankers themselves say. Even Monetarists concede that no limit can be set to the volume of currency put in circulation. If bank deposits are to retain their liquidity, currency must be made available on demand. With regard to deposits, central-bank practitioners have long attempted to dislodge the conventional notion of the deposit-expansion process. In what manner do banks supply deposits? With regard to demand and savings deposits, banks passively accept all payments paid in at a fixed, zero or nonpositive rate of interest. So long as the central bank has a monopoly of the supply of legal tender currency, banks in turn will need to ensure the convertibility of their deposits into cash and, therefore, will need to hold currency in their tills and hold balances with the central bank. And so long as there is a demand to borrow the currency notes issued by the central bank, the central bank will be able to influence the general level of money-market interest rates.

In the United Kingdom, the recent joint memorandum by the Treasury and the Bank of England on monetary control emphasized that the control over the money supply operates indirectly, by influencing the public's demand for money, and not by directly controlling the supply (Monetary Control, 1980). Because of the development of liability management by the commercial banks, it has become more difficult for the central bank to shift the relative pattern of interest rates in such a way as to make holding deposits with the Banking System more or less attractive (Goodhart, 1984). In the United States, Federal Reserve officials have long insisted that the Fed in fact follows a money-market strategy. The operational directives of the Open-Market committee specify values within some range of money-market variables that the manager of the account is to attempt to maintain. The amount of marginal reserves to be furnished and the money-market rates sought are chosen so as to influence the direction and rate of change of a number of more remote intermediate monetary aggregates.[9]

> "The idea of a regular injection of reserves . . . suffers from a naive assumption that the banking system only expands loans after the system (or market factors) have put reserves in the banking system. . . . In any given statement week, the reserves required to be maintained by the banking system are predetermined by the level of deposits existing two weeks earlier. Since excess reserves in the banking system normally run at frictional level . . . the level of total reserves in any given statement week is also pretty well determined in advance. Since banks have to meet their reserve requirements each week (after allowance for carryover privileges), and since they can do nothing within that week to affect required reserves, that total amount of reserves has to be available to the banking system. The Federal Reserve does have discretion as to how the banks can acquire this predetermined level of needed reserves. The reserves can be supplied from the combination of open market operations and the movement of other reserve factors, or they can come from member bank borrowing at the discount window . . . the suggestion that open market operations should be used in the short run to prevent a rise in total reserves through member bank borrowing is completely illogical. Within a statement week, the reserves have to be there; and, in one way or

another, the Federal Reserve will have to accommodate the need for them" (Holmes, 1969, p. 73; see also Burns, 1974; Volcker, 1978; Meek, 1982; Goodhart, 1984).[10]

The second sort of empirical evidence on the endogeneity of the high-powered base comes from formal causality tests between bank reserves and bank deposits. To satisfy Granger causality, R is said to cause M if past values of R can be used to obtain more accurate forecasts of future values of M that those forecasts formed by using only past values of M (Granger, 1969). Sims developed an important procedure for testing Granger causality conditions. The method involves regressing current values of each of the variables on future, current, and past values of the other variable, after both variables have been appropriately prefiltered in order to eliminate serial correlation in the regression residuals (Sims, 1972). Causality running from the dependent variable is indicated when the increment to R^2 from including future values of the independent variable is sufficient to reject the null hypothesis that all future coefficients are zero. The procedure is then repeated, reversing the dependent and independent variables.

Using weekly data, Feige and McGee found that the money stock (*M1*) was exogenous with respect to reserves for both the seven-year period before and after the imposition of lagged reserve accounting in 1968 (Feige and McGee, 1977). In contrast, one-way causality from money to reserves was established in both periods, although the null hypothesis could only be rejected at the ten percent level for the earlier period. Feige and McGee conclude that their results "raise serious doubts about the Fed's use of the traditional reserve-multiplier mechanism to control the money supply. Our findings also call into question estimated money supply equations predicted on the assumption of reserve exogeneity" (Feige and McGee, 1977, p. 549).

A recent paper, based on four different causality test procedures, similarly found that the evidence overwhelmingly supported the position that over the period 1973–1981, unidirectional causality ran from each of the four different monetary aggregates to the monetary base, and from commercial bank lending to the monetary aggregates (Moore and Stuttman, 1984).[11]

The third sort of evidence for the endogeneity of the high-powered base is the extent to which changes in the base can be explained statistically by changes in economic variables, in particular by money wages. Several studies have attempted to fit central bank reaction functions related to macroeconomic policy goals such as inflation, unemployment, balance of payments, and interest rates. It has recently been shown that money-wage rates are by far the most significant explanatory variable, with a highly significant positive coefficient. Lagged money-wage rates alone explain 67 percent of the monthly movement in the money stock, and 85 percent of the quarterly movement (Moore, 1979, 1983).

The fourth sort of evidence is the similar behavior of the growth rates of member and nonmember commercial banks in the United States prior to the Monetary Control Act of 1980, which imposed statutory reserve requirements on all depository institutions. Over that period nonmember banks' reserve requirements were set by state banking authorities and were typically lower than those imposed by the Federal Reserve System. More importantly, nonmember banks were not required to hold their reserves with the central bank, but instead could hold them as deposits with correspondent member banks. There was thus no way the Federal Reserve System could restrict the growth of nonmember bank reserves. Since their reserve growth was not exogenously controlled by the central bank, the conventional view would imply that the growth rate of nonmember bank expansion should have been virtually unlimited. While nonmember banks did in fact grow slightly more rapidly than member banks, this can be completely explained by market factors, such as size of bank and location of market area. The rate of growth of all commercial banks, member and nonmember alike, were both determined by endogenous market forces.

6. Credit Markets and the Provision of Liquidity

There is now considerable evidence that over large sectors of the economy, prices are determined as some fairly stable mark-up over historic normal unit costs (Nordhaus, 1972, Coutts, et al, 1978). Keynesians and others argue that the underlying basic rate of inflation is governed by the excess rate of growth of money wages over the rate of growth of average labor productivity. At the same time Monetarists have shown that over the long run, excess growth in the nominal money-stock over the growth of the real productive potential of the economy will also be reflected in the rate of inflation.

These two empirical regularities logically imply that the rate of growth of the nominal money-stock must be closely related statistically to the rate of growth of money wages (Moore, 1979). Monetarists argue that money-stock changes are exogenously determined by the central bank, and that excess money growth causes money wages to rise, like any other price. Post-Keynesians argue that money-wage growth is more nearly exogneous, and the central bank is viewed as forced to accommodate to money-wage increases to prevent unemployment rates from rising to politically unacceptable levels. The country is then in effect on a wage standard. But, as stated, until post-Keynesians are able to specify more closely the mechanism by which changes in money wages influence the money stock, they like the Monetarists are similarly open to the accusation of having a "Black Box."[12]

The process of monetary accommodation, the validation of money-wage increases which the data reveal, is mistakenly viewed, by both Monetarists and post-Keynesians alike, as the result of a process of *active* policy intervention by the central bank. The notion appears to be that the monetary authorities keep their eyes focused on the state of the economy and interest rates in general, and on the level of unemployment in particular. Whenever unemployment rates approach politically unacceptable levels, the central bank moves to provide additional reserves to accommodate the higher wage and price levels, so as to avoid even higher unemployment.

Such a view overlooks the fact that the central rationale for the creation of central banks, and still by far their most important function, was to provide an elastic currency supply. If financial assets are to possess liquidity, they must be capable of being exchanged quickly, easily, and cheaply into cash. Specialized institutional market-makers, who are willing to buy and sell funds on extremely low margins and who operate with low ratios of equity capital, develop. To ensure the ultimate liquidity of financial assets and so the viability of the financial sysltem, central banks must stand ready to perform the role of lender of last resort. For the system as a whole, as evidenced by the experience of the 1930s, liquidity is determined by what the central bank is willing to purchase. The commercial banking system is the central institution in the liquidity-creating process. As a result, by far the most basic obligation of all monetary authorities is to support, maintain, and encourage orderly conditions in financial markets generally and in the commercial banking system in particular.

In both the United States and the United Kingdom, the evidence indicates that annual changes in the volume of bank intermediation are determined primarily by the quantity of bank lending, although changes in bank security holdings and external capital flows play an important short-run role. In both countries, on annual basis, changes in bank loans explain more than 80 percent of the variation in the money stock (Moore, 1979; Moore and Threadgold, 1980; Kaldor, 1982). This is hardly surprising, since bank total assets must equal bank total liabilities, and loans and deposits are by far the most important components of these totals.

It is through the credit markets that the process of monetary accommodation to higher nominal money-wages occurs. The ability of central banks to control the rate of growth of monetary aggregates therefore hinges on their ability to control the rate of growth of bank lending, rather than the monetary base. Once deposits have been created by an act of lending, the central bank must somehow ensure that the required reserves are available at the settlement date. Otherwise the banks, no matter how hard they scramble for funds, could not in the aggregate meet their reserve requirements. With lagged reserve accounting, once loans have been granted and deposits created, the monetary authorities have no choice but to provide the banks with the necessary reserves, if orderly conditions in the financial markets are to be maintained. Their only decision concerns whether funds should be provided by open-market operations, or whether the banks should be driven to the discount window. Even when reserve accounting is made more contemporaneous, as is currently planned for the United States, the fundamental process is unchanged. Once banks have extended credit and created deposits in the process, the central bank has no choice but to make reserves available, at some price, on demand.

7. Bank Loans to Commercial and Industrial Corporations

The author has previously attempted to estimate the demand for business loans, the largest of the components of bank credit, for both the United Kingdom and the United States (Moore and Threadgold, 1980; Moore, 1983). Not surprisingly, the controllability of bank lending to business corporations appears distinctly limited. Such lending is largely demand-determined. In the United Kingdom, banks have a long tradition of overdraft facilities. In the United States, the credit crunch of 1966 spurred a widespread move towards formalizing, in a legally obligating manner, the hitherto largely informal credit-line arrangements prevailing between banks and their business customers. Corporations wanted and were willing to pay for legally binding credit lines. Unused bank credit commitments, at about $550 billion, currently exceed the total quantity of demand deposits included in measures of the *M1* money stock.

Banks are typically regarded as oligopolists in lending markets, administratively setting their interest rates in line with the prime rate, which is in turn administratively related to short-term money-market rates. The quantity of bank loans is then determined largely by demand, although banks have some scope for affecting the quantity of loans granted through nonprice terms, e.g., collateral requirements applied to discriminate among the fringe of unsatisfied borrowers. The amount of funds obtained through deposits, after adjustment for the reserves which must be held against them, must be reconciled with the quantity of loans granted by changing other portfolio items in the wholesale markets so as to obtain the least costly mix of managed liabilities.[13]

The Monetarist view of monetary endogeneity regards the supply of nominal deposits as being responsive to the public's demand for money, given short-term rates of interest, prices, and income. The present view emphasizes the factors governing the supply of nominal money rather than the demand. Banks attempt to maximize profits by satisfying the public's demand for loans, with funds raised by the least costly mix of retail deposits and managed (wholesale) liabilities. When bank borrowers demand additional bank loans, the public temporarily absorbs the deposits that are created in the process. As a result changes in the supply of money dominate changes in monetary aggregates (Judd and Scadding, 1981; Goodhart, 1984).

Additional bank credit is demanded to finance increases in the value of stocks and work in progress within the production-sales time interval, between the dates of payments for inputs and the dates of receipts from sales revenues.[14] Increases in money-wage rates, the single most important factor cost, and in raw-material costs, will thus lead to an increase in working-capital requirements and the quantity of bank credit demanded, and so to a corresponding increase in bank deposits and in the money stock. Increases in the volume of output, costs remaining unchanged, will similarly require an increase in bank loans to finance the larger value of goods in process, until larger sales receipts cover the additional working-capital finance. If costs or output stabilize at some higher level, the level of bank borrowing will also stabilize at a new higher level.

The amount which working-capital needs increase in response to an increase in costs will vary among individual firms, and will depend on the length of time before output prices are raised in response to higher historic costs. The length of the production period will ordinarily set a plausible lower limit to this time lag. Workers, other factor suppliers, and even customers provide companies with some interest-free, short-term working-capital finance, depending on wage-payment periods, trade credit-terms, and prepayment conventions. But such finance ordinarily is very short compared with the total production period, over which such working-capital needs must be financed at a profit if the company is to remain in business.

Banks set the prime rate and then attempt to meet the loan demand that results. If the resulting demand for credit exceeds the banks' available supply of funds, they must either raise the prime rate or change the degree to which they ration funds (Moore and Threadgold, 1980; Moore 1983).

The estimating procedure followed was, first, to develop a basic equation relating increases in commercial and industrial borrowing to increases in company working-capital needs and, then, to test for the significance of additional variables. Because of the different time periods over which various costs enter the production and pricing process (Coutts et al, 1978), working-capital needs were broken down into the following four components: 1.) employment costs, 2.) materials costs, 3.) stockbuilding costs, and 4.) corporate-tax payments.

It is only increases in costs which generate demand for additional working-capital finance, since existing levels are assumed to be fully financed out of current sales' proceeds. In consequence all explanatory variables were entered as first differences. All variables were entered for both the current and preceding quarters, as suggested by the price mark-up literature.

The initial equation to be tested was as follows:

$$\begin{aligned} TLCIC_t = a_0 &+ a_1\Delta WBill_t + a_2\Delta WBILL_{t-1} + a_3\Delta MBill_t \\ &+ a_4\Delta MBill_{t-1} + a_5\Delta PS_t + a_6\Delta PS_{t-1} + a_7\Delta TBill_t \\ &+ a_8\Delta TBill_{t-1} \end{aligned} \tag{1.3}$$

where

TLCIC = bank loans to commercial and industrial corporations (CICs),
WBill = a proxy for the wage bill of CICs,
MBill = a proxy for the materials costs of CICs,
PS = current price value of stock levels of CICs,
TBill = corporate-tax payments by CICs, and
Δ = quarterly change.

This equation succeeded in explaining from one-half to two-thirds of the total variation in commercial and industrial borrowing in the United States and the United Kingdom countries. Lagged changes in the tax bill and in stock-building were not always significant. On dropping all insignificant variables, a basic equation was selected. Each working-capital variable was highly significant. The magnitude of the coefficients on the wages and materials components of working-capital needs were not significantly different from unity. These coefficients suggest that bank borrowing by CICs increases typically on a one-for-one basis with their requirements for additional working-capital (Moore and Threadgold, 1980; Moore 1983).

Several attempts were made to introduce interest-rate terms, both nominal and real, but most of the results were unsatisfactory. The coefficient on nominal interest-rates was typically positive, due possibly to a positive expectations effect. When the change in real interest-rates was entered, its coefficient was negative and weakly significant. The implied interest-elasticity, calculated at the mean values, was less than −0.1 in both countries.

To the extent CIC borrowing is primarily for working-capital purposes, this very low implied interest-elasticity is not surprising.[15] Taken at face value, the results imply that the ability of the monetary authorities to restrain the growth of company borrowing indirectly, by varying short-term interest rates, is severely limited.[16] In the short-run, loan demand appears largely insensitive to interest cost variations.[17]

The attempt to capture changes in credit rationing was modeled by the use of dummy variables to measure any special characteristics of credit-crunch periods. Several but not all such dummies had negative coefficients, as expected, but none approached statistical significance. To the extent discretionary credit rationing was directed by banks primarily at loans to persons, real estate, and other financial companies, these results for CICs are perhaps not too surprising.

In conclusion, for both the United States and the United Kingdom it was possible to identify a single equation for bank business lending that had a relatively high degree of explanatory power. The implicit assumption of the analysis was that banks set their lending rates, and then attempt to meet the demand for loans that results. There was no evidence that changes in the degree to which banks ration credit were important. The monetary authorities' ability to control the expansion of bank credit is primarily through their ability to influence the levels of short-term interest rates. The low interest-elasticity of real lending rates, and the failure of nominal rates to be significant and negatively signed, suggests that the banking authorities' power to control the volume of credit expansion through this means is slight, particularly over the short run.

8. Summary

The historical evidence suggests that in both the United States and the United Kingdom the ability of the monetary authorities to restrict the rate of bank credit expansion is severely limited. The growth of money-wage rates, both as a component of companies' demand for working-capital finance and as determinants of disposable personal income, appears to play the most important role in determining the demand for bank credit.

Since central banks, as consistent with their paramount supportive role to the financial system, operate to allow the money stock to accommodate increases in the demand for bank credit, monetary aggregates may properly be considered to move endogenously. Monetarists are not justified in regarding the money stock as in practice an exogenous variable, simply because it appears in principle under the control of monetary authorities. The economics profession in general must come around to the view that the supply of money is horizontal at every going short-term interest rate. Bank reserves cannot be quantitatively constrained if deposits are to retain their liquidity. The quantity of money is always demand-determined, so that there is never an excess supply of nominal money balances. Central banks, within limits set by the level of foreign interest-rates and the degree of international capital mobility, are only able to determine the short-term interest rate at which they are willing to supply legal-tender liquidity. Unless they attempt to control bank credit expansion directly and quantitatively, the money stock is not a control variable.

On the basis of the historical record for both the United States and the United Kingdom at least since the mid-1960s, the money stock varies endogenously, and the single most important determinant appears to be the behavior of money wages. As a result it is extremely difficult for central banks to restrict the rate of monetary growth when money wages and incomes are rising rapidly.

Accommodative central-bank behavior, with its focus on maintaining some administered level of interest rates, is a logical necessity derived from the nature of money and liquidity in all credit-money economies.

Notes

1. The usefulness of the Quantity Theory as a policy guide stands or falls on the proposition that the demand for money, or its reciprocal, the income velocity of money, is stable and largely invariant to changes in the quantity of money. For if this were not so, and velocity were purely a statistical residual relationship, as the Radcliffe committee suggested, control over the quantity of money would then have no *causal* influence on the level of money expenditures (Kaldor, 1982).

2. In the case of the United Kingdom, it is conceded that the working arrangements with the discount houses prevent the Bank of England from exercising rigid monetary-base control. But these institutional arrangements could be changed, and alternative procedures assuring reasonable control of the money stock envisaged (Monetary Control, 1980).

3. The price level in Spain approximately doubled between 1550 and 1600 (Hamilton, 1934).

4. An important exception was the high level of excess reserves held by commercial banks in the United States during the 1930s. See Friedman and Schwartz (1963).

5. Wicksell himself was concerned to explain the long-run fall in prices during the 20 years preceding his writing of *Interest and Prices* (1898). His answer was to emphasize the importance of what he termed the natural rate of interest, or what is now called the real return on investment, i.e., the productivity, in terms of real goods, of the inputs on which the borrowed

money is to be spent. Wicksell believed that there had been a fall in the natural rate over this period, and that the Banking System had failed to allow interest rates to fall sufficiently. Wicksell argued that when the actual (or market) rate of interest is above the natural rate, the growth of credit, money, and prices will fall; when it is below, the growth of credit, money, and prices will rise. So long as the discrepancy persists, the fall or rise will continue cumulatively (Wicksell, 1907).

Nevertheless, since the natural rate is a real rate, and the market rate is a money rate, as soon as one distinguishes between current prices and expectations of future prices, it is apparent that there will be a whole set of natural rates, each for different equilibria rising or falling price trends. If all prices are equally flexible, there is no way of distinguishing among these equilibria. Myrdal argued that in the real world, wages are less flexible than other prices, and one equilibrium might be regarded as better than another if it put less strain on the less-flexible prices, enabling the economy to function with smaller excesses of supply or demand. In that view, he favored an equilibrium in which money wages moved little, so that with increasing productivity, consumer prices, supposed to be more flexible, fell. This particular Myrdal equilibrium, out of the many Wicksellian equilibria, has to be selected on nonmonetary criteria, depending on the institutional structure of the economy. Depending on circumstances, prices (as represented by some particular price index) may be constant, falling, or rising (G. Myrdal, 1933).

6. Friedman and Schwartz have recently argued that the interwar period of the United States, which broadly supports the Keynesian vision, was anomalous in the sense that for the remainder of more than a century of experience, both in the United States and the United Kingdom, the data are more supportive of the Quantity Theory (Friedman and Schwartz, 1982).

7. Interestingly enough, in the *Treatise* Keynes recognized clearly that the nominal money stock responded endogenously to the increased working capital demands associated with an increase in investment spending and an expansion of output. In his stylized model, "An Exercise in the Pure Theory of the Credit Cycle," he assumed explicitly that "the banks create just enough additional money for the industrial circulation, after allowing for any fluctuations in the amount of financial circulation to allow the absorption of the unemployed factors of production into employment at a steady rate.... This amounts to the banks supplying the entrepreneurs with whatever they require, over and above their profits, to pay wages on the gradually increasing scale which is assumed and to increase their business deposits" (*Treatise*, 1930, p. 275).

8. In both the United States and the United Kingdom, total bank debt in existence at any time characteristically lies between one-half to two-thirds of the total amount of outstanding lines of credit and overdraft facilities which have been formally committed (Federal Reserve Board, 1980; Monetary Control, 1980).

9. Central bankers insist that in the short run, money-stock creation is a joint result of a complex interaction among households, business corporations, financial institutions, the Treasury, and the central bank. In addition they emphasize that most of the reported short-term movements in monetary aggregates are primarily the result of statistical *noise*—random forces and estimating errors in the data. "It is clear that, as a matter of fact, the Federal Reserve does not attempt to increase the money supply by a given amount in any period by furnishing a fixed amount of reserves on the assumption that they would be multiplied to result in a given increase in money" (Maisel, 1969, p. 161). If the Fed never regards itself as in practice determining changes in monetary aggregates over the short run, it is hard to see how it can be viewed as determining changes over longer runs, which are simply aggregations of shorter runs.

10. Since October 1979, the Federal Reserve has professed that its actions are directed to achieving a desired rate of growth of specified monetary aggregates, and that it is no longer

following a money-market strategy. Under the old approach the trading desk in New York operated day-to-day and week-to-week to hold the Federal funds rate within a narrow band. The Federal funds rate target and changes in this objective were determined with a view to induce the desired money-growth rates. Since October 1979, the desk's week-to-week objective has been set in terms of reserves. Under the new approach the desk aims to supply reserves at a level consistent with the money growth objectives set by the Federal Open Market Committee (FOMC). The interest rate band has been widened.

Nevertheless since that date, actual grwoth rates of the high-powered base and monetary aggregates have been extremely unstable, and have been clearly *positively* correlated with fluctuations in short-term interest rates. This strongly suggests that current (post-1979) practices of the Federal Reserve continue to involve a blend of money market considerations. The Fed has acknowledged that the FOMC continues to set broad ranges of tolerance for money-market interest rates. It argues however that these ranges no longer serve as rigid constraints (Volker 1978; Judd and Scadding 1981; Meek, 1982).

11. The only exception was a bidirectional or feedback relationship found to exist between the monetary base and the *M2* aggregate (Moore and Stuttman, 1984, pp. 13–17).

12. The post-Keynesian view that changes in the money stock are determined fundamentally by the rate of growth of money wages does explain why in virtually all countries the rate of money growth was so much higher during the 1970s than during the 1960s. If money growth were truly exogenous, this growth somehow would have to be attributed to massive and at the same time coincident errors by different monetary authorities.

13. Historically, imbalances between changes in loans and deposits were financed by changes in marketable securities, primarily central-government debt. Since 1962 the development of an active market in negotiable certificates of deposits (CDs) has enabled banks to place large quantities of these liabilities at their own initiative. This liability management has enabled banks to run down their precautionary reserves and to rely on liability-side liquidity to meet demands for funds. As a result they have been better able to accommodate changes in the demand for loans (Judd and Scadding, 1981; Goodhart, 1984).

14. Production takes time, and time must be taken seriously. In modern economies, production costs normally are incurred and paid prior to the receipt of sales proceeds. Such costs represent a working-capital investment by the firm, for which it must necessarily obtain finance. Over wide sectors of the economy, prices are administered as some fairly stable mark-up over historical normal unit-costs (Coutts et al, 1978). Whenever wage or raw-material price increases raise current production costs, unchanged production flows will require additional working-capital finance. In the absence of instantaneous replacement cost pricing, firms must finance their increased working-capital needs by increasing their borrowings from their banks or by running down their liquid assets.

Working-capital needs may also be met by increasing nonbank short-term borrowing, increasing long-term debt issues, raising additional equity finance internally or externally, or realizing nonliquid assets. Each of these sources of funds typically takes longer to arrange. In the U.K. study, alternative definitions of the dependent variable were tried in an attempt to specify the extent to which companies would increase bank loans or draw down their banks deposits or other liquid assets to meet increases in their working-capital requirements. Somewhat surprisingly, gross bank-borrowing was more closely determined by changes in working-capital needs than either of the net definitions (Moore and Threadgold, 1980).

15. It is generally believed that CICs also borrow from banks to finance fixed-investment expenditures as well as working-capital needs, at least temporarily until they have arranged sufficient longer-term financing. The inclusion of a term representing changes in current price,

corporate fixed-investment (predominantly CICs) proved insignificant and its coefficient had the wrong sign.

16. It is however probable that variations in the cost of borrowing may have strong effects which could not be caught by this simple single-equation, reduced-form approach. High interest costs induce companies to lower their demand for working capital by directly cutting back on their wage and materials bills, thus reducing their volume of employment, production, and inventories of goods in process. Such effects could only be caught by a simultaneous-equation system, in which interest rates were allowed to affect the various uses for working-capital finance.

17. The failure to find larger and more significant interest-rate effects may be due to the unwillingness of these central banks to permit wider short-run fluctuations in the level of interest rates over much of the period. Positive coefficients on nominal interest rates alternatively may be due to a positive expectations effect, in which current rises in rates lead to expectations of further future increases.

References

Burns, A. 1974. Statement Before the Committee on Banking and Currency, House of Representatives, 30 July 1974. *Federal Reserve Bulletin*, 60, August.

Cagan, P. 1965. *Determinants and Effects of Changes in the Stock of Money*. New York, Columbia University Press.

Coutts, K.; Goldley, W.; and Nordhaus W. 1978. *Industrial Pricing in the United Kingdom*. Cambridge, Cambridge University Press.

Federal Reserve Board. 1980. *Statistical Release, Loan Commitments at Selected Large Commercial Banks, G21*. September.

Feige, E. and McGee, R. 1977. Money Supply Control and Lagged Reserve Accounting. *Journal of Money, Credit and Banking*, November.

Friedman, M. and Meiselman, D. 1963. The Relative Stability of Monetary Velocity and the Investment Multiplier in the United States 1898–1958. In: *Commission on Money and Credit Stabilization Policies*. Englewood Cliffs, NJ, Prentice-Hall.

Friedman, M. and Schwartz, A. 1963. *A Monetary History of the United States 1869–1960*. Princeton, Princeton University Press.

Friedman, M. and Schwartz, A. 1982. *Monetary Trends in the United States and the United Kingdom*. Chicago, University of Chicago Press.

Goodhart, C. A. E. 1984. *Monetary Theory and Practice*. London, MacMillan.

Granger, C. 1969. Investigating Causal Relations by Econometric Models and Cross-Spectral Methods. *Econometrica*, July.

Hamilton, E. 1934. *American Treasure and the Price Revolution in Spain*. Cambridge, MA, Harvard University Press.

Hicks, Sir J. 1977. *Economic Perspectives: Further Essays on Money and Growth*. Oxford, Oxford University Press.

Holmes, A. 1969. Operational Constraints on the Stabilization of Money Supply Growth. *Controlling Monetary Aggregates*, Federal Reserve Bank of Boston, June.

Hume, D. 1955. *Writings on Economics*. E. Rotwein (ed), Madison, WI, University of Wisconsin Press.

Judd, J. and Scadding, J. 1981. Liquidity Management, Bank Loans, and Deposit Market Disequilibrium. *Economic Review*, Federal Reserve Bank of San Francisco, Summer.

Kaldor, N. 1982. *The Scourge of Monetarism*. Oxford, Oxford University Press.

Keynes, J. M. 1930. *A Treatise on Money*. London, Macmillan.

Laidler, D. 1981. Monetarism: An Interpretation and An Appraisal. In: *Economic Journal*, March.

Lombra, R. and Torto, R. 1973. Federal Reserve Defensive Behavior and the Reverse Causation Argument. *Southern Economic Journal*, July.

Maisel, S. 1969. Controlling Monetary Aggregates. *Controlling Monetary Aggregates*, Federal Reserve Bank of Boston, June.

Meek, P. 1982. *U.S. Monetary Policy and Financial Markets*. Federal Reserve Bank of New York.

Monetary Control. 1980. London, HMSO, March.

Moore, B. J. 1979. The Endogenous Money Stock. *Journal of Post-Keynesian Economics*, Fall.

Moore, B. J. 1983. Unpacking the Post-Keynesian Black Box: Ban Lending and the Money Supply. *Journal of Post-Keynesian Economics*, Summer.

Moore, B. J. and Threadgold, A. 1980. *Bank Lending and the Money Supply*. Bank of England Discussion Paper no. 10. Boston, Bank of New England, July.

Moore, B. J. and Stuttman, S. 1984. A Causality Analysis of the Determinants of Money Growth. *British Review of Economic Issues*, Summer.

Myrdal, G. 1933. *Monetary Equilibrium*. London, Hodge. (English translation, 1939.)

Nordhaus, W. 1972. Recent Developments in Price Dynamics. In: *The Econometrics of Price Determination*, O. Eckstein (ed.), Washington, Board of Governors of the Federal Reserve.

Radcliffe Committee. 1959. *Committee on the Working of the Monetary System*, London, HMSO.

Sims, C. 1972. Money, Income and Causality. *American Economic Review*, September.

Tobin, J. 1981. The Monetarist Counter-Revolution Today—An Appraisal. *Economic Journal*, March.

Volker, P. 1978. The Role of Monetary Targets in an Age of Inflation. *Journal of Monetary Economics*, April.

Wicksell, K. 1907. The Influence of the Rate of Interest on Prices. *Economic Journal*, June.

Wills, H. R. 1982. The Simple Economics of Bank Regulation. *Economica*. August.

Wojnilower, A. 1980. *The Central Role of Credit Crunches in Recent Financial History. Brookings Papers on Economic Activity*, no. 2.

2 THE DEMAND CURVE FOR MONEY FURTHER CONSIDERED

Leonard Forman, Miles Groves, and Alfred S. Eichner

1. Introduction

The convention in economics is to assume that what is termed the money stock—currency plus checkable deposits—is a variable which is exogenously controlled by the monetary authorities. This assumption makes it possible to assert that a change in one or more economic variables, including the short-term interest rate, influences the "demand" for money. It is on this basis that a demand curve for money is usually specified and, if the study is an empirical one, the parameters of that money-demand equation estimated.

Cooley and LeRoy (1981), in a review of the econometric evidence from numerous studies, report they were unable to confirm that the demand for money depends "negatively on a short-term interest rate, representing a proxy for the opportunity cost of holding money. . . . " The parameter estimates vary so widely and depend so critically on what other variables are included as arguments within the function as to raise doubt that a stable demand curve for money actually exists. Indeed, Judd and Scadding (1982), acknowledging this point, have offered an explanation of why the demand curve for money must have shifted over time.

Cooley and LeRoy chose to focus on the econometric issues raised by the disparate results from empirical studies of the demand for money, and did not pursue their observation that perhaps the theory itself ought to be re-examined. This article picks up on the latter point, arguing that the specification of separate supply and demand curves for money is the wrong way to model the United States or any other economy with a minimally advanced monetary and financial system. The argument can be summarized as follows:

First, the amount of bank reserves, and thus the monetary base, is not the exogenously determined variable assumed in both orthodox Keynesian and monetarist models but instead depends on the level of nominal income. This is because the central bank, in order to maintain the liquidity of the financial system, is forced to purchase government securities in the open market so as to accommodate, at least in part, the need for additional credit as the pace of economic activity quickens. With the amount of unborrowed bank reserves, and thus the monetary base, to a significant extent endogenously determined, it follows that the money supply is, to no less an extent, endogenously determined as well. It is therefore a misspecification to assume that the money stock, or any of its components, is entirely exogenous, subject to the control of the monetary authorities, and then to derive a demand curve for money based on that assumption. In reality, the demand for and supply of "money" are interdependent, with no possibility in practice of being able to distinguish between the two.

Second, it is the demand for credit rather than the demand for money which is the necessary starting point for analyzing the role played by monetary factors in determining the level of real economic activity. This demand for credit consists of the demand for business loans and the demand for consumer loans, and it can be compared to the lending capacity of the commercial banking system, as measured by total bank deposits (demand and time deposits), to indicate the degree of liquidity pressure. The resulting ratio, L, can then be shown to be the most significant monetary determinant of durable goods purchases, and thus of the level of real economic activity itself—even more important than any long-term interest rate. It is therefore the ratio of bank loans to bank deposits as a measure of liquidity pressure, and thus of disequilibrium within the monetary-financial system, rather than just the amount of bank deposits (which, together with the amount of currency in circulation, is usually identified as the money stock) that influences the level of real economic activity.

These conclusions are based on the empirical evidence obtained in estimating the parameters of a post-Keynesian short-period model of the United States economy as an alternative to more conventional Keynesian and monetarist models (Eichner, 1979; Forman and Eichner, 1981; Forman, Groves, and Eichner, 1983), and they are supported by that empirical evidence. In section 2, the evidence that the Federal Reserve Board's (the Fed's) open-market operations are, to a significant extent, endogenously determined will be presented. In section 3 the causal sequence by which a nonaccommodating monetary policy by the Fed leads to a change in the level of real economic activity without the stock of money playing any direct role will be outlined and, again, some evidence presented. Finally, in section 4, a brief comment will be made about the role of the money stock in determining the secular rise in the price level.

2. The Determinants of Open-Market Operations

It is usually assumed that a change in the Fed's holdings of government securities will lead to a change, with the same sign attached, in the reserves of the commercial banking system. It was the failure to observe this relationship empirically[1] which led us, in constructing the monetary-financial block of our model, to try to find some other way of representing the effect of the Fed's open-market operations on the Banking System. The alternative approach finally adopted consists of viewing the Federal Reserve System as an integral part of the overall banking and financial system and only secondarily concerned with achieving certain macroeconomic targets, such as a high growth of real output and price stability.[2]

Within this framework, the relationship between the Fed's open-market operations and the reserves of the commercial banking system can be brought out by means of the accounting identity which applies to the Federal Reserve System's sources and uses of funds. The accounting identity is as follows:

$$FGS + ResB + \text{Other Sources (Assets)} = ResT + Cur + \text{Other Uses (Liabilities)} \tag{2.1}$$

where *FGS* is the Fed's holdings of government securities; *ResB* is the commercial banking system's borrowed reserves (advances and discounts); *ResT* is the commercial banking system's total reserves; and *Cur* is the amount of currency in circulation, that is, the amount of currency held by the public, *CurP*, plus the amount of currency held by banks as vault cash, *CurB*. The Federal Reserve System's other sources of funds, or assets, consist of 1.) acceptances; 2.) float; 3.) gold stock; 4.) Treasury currency outstanding; and 5.) other assets. The Federal Reserve System's other uses of funds, or liabilities, consist of 1.) Treasury cash holdings; 2.) deposits at the Fed by the Treasury, foreigners, and others; and 3.) other liabilities.

Since the monetary base, *MB*, is equal to total bank reserves, *ResT*, plus currency in circulation, *Cur*, the above identity can be written as follows in first difference form with the change in the monetary base isolated on the left-hand side:

$$\Delta MB = \Delta FGS + \Delta ResB + \Delta\text{Other Sources} - \Delta\text{Other Uses} \quad (2.2)$$

or, with the components of the monetary base delineated,

$$\Delta ResNB + \Delta ResB + \Delta CurP = \\ \Delta FGS + \Delta ResB + \Delta\text{Other Sources} - \Delta\text{Other Uses} \quad (2.3)$$

where *ResNB* is the commercial banking system's nonborrowed reserves which, since 1961, include the currency held by banks as vault cash. Subtracted $\Delta ResB$ and $\Delta CurP$ from both sides of equation 2.3 yields the following:

$$\Delta ResNB = \Delta FGS - \Delta CurP + \Delta FdA \quad (2.4)$$

where ΔFdA, or the net change in the Fed's assets, is the term (ΔOther Sources $-$ ΔOther Uses).

What equation 2.4 brings out is that a change in the amount of currency held by the public or any of the items included among the Fed's other assets represents a flow of funds either into or out of the Federal Reserve System, depending on the item and the sign attached to it, and that unless the Fed offsets this flow through the purchase or sale of government securities, the nonborrowed reserves of the commercial banking system will, as a result, change. Thus, in the face of a fluctuating public demand for currency, flows of gold into and out of the country, variations in the amount of deposits held at the Fed by foreigners and others, changes in the amount of float and fluctuations in the Treasury's cash holdings, the Fed must engage in open-market operations just to maintain bank reserves at a given level. This is the neutralizing component of a fully accommodating policy, and it is one reason why it is so difficult in practice to relate the change in bank reserves to open-market operations. The other component of such a policy is the accommodating piece itself.

An increase in the demand for credit will, to the extent it is satisfied, lead to an increase in bank deposits (especially demand deposits). This is because banks make loans by simply crediting the borrower's account at the bank with the amount of funds being advanced. The increase in deposits will, however, require that banks maintain larger reserves at the Fed. Thus required reserves, *ResR*, will increase and, unless the Fed acts through the purchase of government securities in the open market to provide banks with the necessary additional reserves, banks will find themselves with insufficient reserves to meet their legal requirements. While both the Fed's own discount window and the federal funds market will provide some temporary relief (along with the system of delayed reserve accounting),[3] the fact is that, unless the Fed provides the additional reserves, the Banking System can quickly become illiquid, with banks unable to convert the government securities they hold as secondary reserves into additional legal reserves (or cash) and indeed unable to make any further loans. If a significant portion of the nonfinancial institutions' outstanding debt needs to be rolled over, the inability of the banks to provide additional credit may lead to a rapid fall in the value of assets as those turned down for loans seek to raise funds instead through the sale of their assets, and a serious financial crisis may then ensue (Minsky, 1982). It is to prevent this type of situation from occurring (or, if it should occur, as in 1969, to prevent it from worsening) that the Fed is forced to accommodate, at least in part, whatever demand for credit may manifest itself.

A fully accommodating change in the Fed's holdings of government securities, $\Delta FGSA$, can therefore be specified as follows:

$$\Delta FGSA = -\Delta FdA + \Delta CurP + \Delta ResR \qquad (2.5)$$

Equation 2.5 implies that the Fed's open-market operations, as measured by the change in its holdings of government securities, depend on a set of factors that reflect the changing level of economic activity, and that the Fed's open-market operations are, to this extent, endogenously determined. Empirical support for this proposition can be found by regressing the actual change in the Fed's holdings of government securities, using the quarterly data available for 1953 through 1978, against the three right-hand-side variables in equation 2.5. The results are shown in Table 2–1. For the period as a whole, approximately four-fifths of the quarterly change in the Fed's holdings of government securities is accounted for by these three explanatory variables.[4] The evidence, then, is that the Fed's open-market operations are, to a considerable extent, endogenously determined.

Indeed, only a portion of the total change in the Fed's holdings of government securities can be considered to be exogenous—and only a portion of that can be considered the result of a deliberate policy decision. The portion which is exogenous is that represented by the difference between the total change in the Fed's holdings of government securities and the change that would be required, based on equation 2.5, to fully accommodate the current demand for credit. That is,

$$\Delta FGSD = \Delta FGST - (-\Delta FdA + \Delta CurP + \Delta ResR) \qquad (2.6)$$

where $\Delta FGSD$ is that portion of the total, or actual, change in the Fed's holdings of government securities, $\Delta FGST$, which is not endogenously determined and which can thus be viewed as being exogenous. Only a portion

Table 2-1. Variables Affecting the Federal Reserve Board's Open-Market Operations (As Measured by FGS)

variables	*interval*	*1953–1978*	*1953–1961*	*1962–1978*	*1962–1972*	*1972–1978*
FdA	*coeff*	−.76	−.66	−.77	−.64	−.81
	t ratio	14.84	6.70	12.10	6.35	8.39
Res_R	*coeff*	.75	.35	.81	.61	2
	t ratio	6.89	2.79	5.58	4.15	3.88
	coeff	1.10	1.42	1.04	.90	1.17

CurP	*t ratio*	14.00	3.74	8.40	3.65	3.14
Const	*coeff*	25.37	−24.89	82.12	230.08	−169.91
	t ratio	.35*	.55*	.56*	1.42*	.28*
R^2		.80	.63	.74	.60	.76
D-W		2.95	2.22	3.12	2.22	3.57
Observations		104	36	68	44	28

*Not statistically significant at 5 percent level of probability.

of that exogenously determined change in the Fed's holdings of government securities can be considered to be the result of a deliberate policy decision, however. The rest will reflect the Fed's inability to correctly anticipate the actual change in all the relevant variables, and thus must be treated as an error factor. That is,

$$\Delta FGSD = XM1 + Err \tag{2.7}$$

where $XM1$ is a policy variable reflecting a decision by the Fed either not to fully accommodate the demand for credit (when its sign is negative) or to accommodate the demand for credit more than is necessary (when the sign is positive). Still, the important point is not how much of the exogenously determined change in the Fed's holdings of government securities reflects a deliberate policy decision and how much is inadvertent.[5] The effect, in either case, will be the same—a change in free reserves, or the amount of nonborrowed reserves in excess of required reserves, equal to $\Delta FGSD$.[6] The important point is rather that most of the change in the Fed's holdings of government securities during any given quarter will, as indicated by the regression results shown in Table 2–1, be an endogenous response to the changing demand for credit.

If the change in the Fed's holdings of government securities (through its open-market operations) is, to a considerable extent, endogenously determined, it follows that bank reserves, too, are similarly endogenous. This conclusion, if confirmed by other empirical studies, has two implications.

First, models which assume bank reserves to be entirely exogenous are misspecified, and any empirical results based on such models are suspect. The same, of course, is true of models which assume that either the monetary base or the money stock itself are exogenous, since bank reserves are the putatively exogenous component of those larger aggregates.

Second, the demand for money (or some other monetary aggregate) cannot be distinguished empirically from the supply by assuming that economic factors impact only on the former and not on the latter. Again, any empirical results based on such a formulation are suspect.

These implications of the Fed's open-market operations, and hence bank reserves, being to a considerable extent endogenously determined thus place in a somewhat different light Cooley and LeRoy's report that they were unable to confirm, after examining the econometric evidence, the existence of a demand curve for money as that function is usually specified. The theory cannot be confirmed because it is most likely incorrect.

The empirical work we have done in estimating the parameters of our model not only casts doubt on the existence of a separate demand curve for money, it also raises the question of whether the money stock—however that aggregate is defined—is the crucial variable linking the Fed's open-market operations to a change in the level of real economic activity, such as the conventional IS-LM models would suggest.

3. Monetary Policy and Economic Activity

Earlier work on the model had already suggested that the most important monetary-financial determinants of real economic activity, at least over the cycle, were two-fold. First, and foremost, was the degree of liquidity pressure, as measured by the ratio of bank loans to bank deposits and, second, the cyclical movement of two long-term interest rates, the yield on high-grade corporate bonds, and the mortgage rate (Forman and Eichner, 1981). In constructing the monetary-financial block of our model, it was therefore necessary only to explain the process by which these two sets of variables were determined, and the role, if any, the various monetary aggregates, such as the monetary base or *M1* and *M2*, played in the process.

The degree of liquidity pressure, L, is defined in the model as the ratio of bank loans—consumer as well as business loans—to bank deposits. The numerator thus reflects the demand for credit, while the denominator measures the lending capacity of the commercial banking system as determined by its deposit inflows. When the former increases relative to the latter, the commercial banking system will become less liquid and thus less capable of providing credit.

The demand for credit over the cycle can, in turn, be explained largely by the cyclical movement in real economic activity, reflecting the working-capital needs of business and the consumer durable financing needs of households. The demand for credit would appear to be insensitive to the cyclical movement in interest rates—although the amount of business loans will be affected, on the supply side, by the shift in the loan portfolios of financial institutions caused, among other factors, by a movement of the commercial-paper rate relative to the prime rate (Forman, Groves, and Eichner, 1983).

Normally an increase in the demand for credit will lead to a corresponding increase in the deposits of the commercial banking system, leaving the ratio of loans to deposits for the most part unchanged. (Any cyclical movement in economic activity, because of its effect on the cash balances of different sectors, will alter this ratio slightly.) However, the rise in deposits will at the same time lead to an increase in the commercial banking system's required reserves. If the Fed responds by providing additional reserves (that is, if it pursues a fully accommodating policy with both *XM1* and *Err* equal to zero), no further effect will be felt. But if it acts otherwise, two consequences will follow.

First, the banks will be forced to sell off a portion of the government securities they hold as secondary reserves; this so they can meet the loan commitments they have already made, while they simultaneously act to reduce their future loan commitments. But with the Fed no longer willing to purchase government securities, the banks will be forced to sell to other private parties, and this will have the effect of reducing the amount of deposits within the Banking System as a whole. The banks will therefore find themselves under even greater pressure to curtail their lending activity, leaving them with no choice but to ration credit. Certain types of loans may, in fact, then become unobtainable, forcing nonfinancial institutions to cut back on their discretionary spending for lack of financing. This is why the liquidity-pressure variable, *L*, helps explain the cyclical movement in business investment and other types of durable goods purchases independently of any change in interest rates.

Second, the ratio of free to total reserves, *ResF/ResT*, will decline. The fall in this ratio, together with the simultaneous increase in the degree of liquidity pressure, will lead to a rise in the federal funds rate as banks try to obtain from other sources the reserves which the Fed refuses to provide (except, grudgingly, through the discount window). The rise in the federal funds rate will then be followed, with a lag, by an increase in the other short-term and long-term interest rates—including, most importantly, the yield on high-grade corporate bonds and the mortgage rate. The cyclical rise in the two long-term interest rates will have a further dampening effect on the growth of certain types of durable goods purchases, especially plant and equipment expenditures by small business firms and residential construction.

The empirical evidence in support of the process, or causal sequence, just outlined, whereby a nonaccommodating monetary policy leads to increased liquidity pressure, together with higher long-term interest rates, and thence to a cyclical downturn in real economic activity, will be found in the equations which, as now estimated, constitute the monetary-financial block of the model we are constructing (Forman, Groves, and Eichner, 1983). What is noteworthy about this causal sequence, assuming its existence is confirmed by other econometric studies, is that it makes no mention of the money stock as conventionally defined. With an additional equation to account for the amount of money in circulation, the cyclical movements in *M1* and *M2* can both be determined, since demand deposits and time deposits are otherwise derived within the block (as the denominator of the liquidity-pressure variable). However, the sum of the amount of money in circulation plus the amount of demand and time deposits (that is, the money stock as conventionally defined) plays no role in determining either the degree of liquidity pressure or the cyclical movement in long-term interest rates. This is because the money stock as conventionally defined is determined concurrently with, and largely by the same factors as, the degree of liquidity pressure—with the latter variable, and not the money stock, serving as the critical link in the causal sequence.

Some evidence in support of this last proposition will be found in the regression results reported in table 2–2. While the degree of liquidity pressure, *L*, and the ratio of free to total bank reserves, *ResF*/*ResT*, are each significantly correlated with the cyclical movement in the federal funds rate (equations 1 and 2, table 2–2), the same is not true for the cyclical movement of total bank deposits, *Dep*; the cyclical movement of just demand deposits alone, *DD*; or the cyclical movement of the money stock as conventionally defined, *M1* (equations 3, 4, and 5, table 2–2).[7] Moreover, while the degree of liquidity pressure and the ratio of free to total reserves together provide a fairly satisfactory explanation for the cyclical movement in the federal funds rate (eqation 6, table 2–2), replacing either of those two variables with the money stock, *M1*, or even including the latter as an additional argument, does little to improve the equation's explanatory power (equations 7, 8, and 9, table 2–2).[8]

Thus it is possible, in the interest of parsimony, to eliminate the monetary stock, as conventionally defined, from macroeconomic analysis altogether. The way in which monetary factors influence the level of real economic activity can still be explained in a way that is consistent with the empirical evidence. One need only take into account the demand for credit relative to the lending capacity of the commercial banking system. It is the demand for credit which, upon being satisfied by the joint action of the banks and the Fed (the former in actually making the loans and the latter in providing the banks with the required additional reserves), will lead to an increase in bank deposits (and thus to an increase in the money stock, as conventionally defined, while leaving the ratio of bank loans to bank deposits unchanged). Further, it is the demand for credit which, upon *not* being fully accommodated by the Fed and thus creating a disequilibrium condition within the monetary-financial system, will lead to an increase in the ratio of bank loans to bank deposits (while slowing the growth of the money stock, as conventionally defined). The resulting rise in the liquidity-pressure variable, *L*, will not only force banks to ration credit, it, together with the parallel rise in the ratio of free to total reserves, will also lead to higher short-term and long-term interest rates.

One can come closer to bringing out what the focus on the money stock, as

Table 2-2. Variables Affecting the Federal Funds Rate (1960–1978)

	C	*L*	*F/T*	*Dep*	*DD*	*M1*	R^2
	−.25	39.795					
1							.265
	(1.41)	(5.30)					
	−.51		−66.02				
2							.63
	(3.96)		(11.38)				
	.01			−.07			
3							.01
	(.049)			(1.46)			
	.04				−.148		
4							.047
	(.21)				(2.17)		
	.0059					−.125	

5					.022
	(.029)			(1.65)	
6	−.63	31.16	−60.75		.7956
	(6.49)	(7.77)	(13.89)		
7	−.45		−72.54	−.249	.763
	(4.35)		(15.25)	(6.49)	
8	−.312	44.84		.0837	.2669
	(1.677)	(5.069)		(1.075)	
9	−.561	22.467	−65.69	−.13	.8187
	(6.037)	(4.835)	(−14.94)	(3.209)	

Data source: DRI Macro Data Base.

conventionally defined, is meant to illuminate—namely, the availability of the means of payment—by formulating the macroeconomic model within a flow-of-funds framework, as we have done (see Eichner, 1979). In this way, it becomes clear that the availability of the means of payment by each type of nonfinancial institution—business firms, households, nonprofit organizations, governmental units, and the rest of the world—depends first and primarily on its net cash inflow, that is, on its total revenue or income during the period less any cash outlays, and then secondarily on its access to credit—whether a loan has actually been obtained or whether the funds are simply available if needed through a line of bank credit. Within this framework, the focus is on the flow of funds throughout the economy as a whole without any effort to identify any particular stock of monetary assets as the effective constraint on the amount of those funds. The growth in the flow of funds depends solely on the rate at which the commercial banking system is willing to provide credit or additional funds, supported by the willingness of the central bank to provide the necessary increase in bank reserves. The actual amount of bank deposits at any given point in time (along with the amount of currency, or federal reserve notes, the public wishes to hold) is of little consequence. Thus the money stock, as conventionally defined, can for all practical purposes be ignored, greatly simplifying the task of constructing an empirically valid macroeconomic model.

Furthermore, omitting the money stock from the analysis eliminates a basic confusion. The Fed's open-market operations affect the rest of the monetary-financial sector and the real sector through a change in bank deposits relative to bank loans, rather than a change in deposits alone. It is the ratio of loans to deposits, interpreted as measuring the degree of liquidity pressure, which serves as the causal link.

Eliminating the money stock from the model has a further advantage in that it avoids any need to distinguish the demand for money from supply. It also renders moot the question of how the money stock is to be defined, thus avoiding another issue that has made empirical research more difficult. Indeed, the only disadvantage is that it would mean abandoning the IS = LM framework, which has dominated macroeconomics ever since the Hicks-Hansen interpretation of the *General Theory* became the prevailing one. But then that might not be such a disadvantage (Eichner, 1977).

4. Money Supply and the Price Level

Monetarists will, of course, object that eliminating the money stock from the macro model will leave the secular rise in the price level unexplained. While a more complete response to this objection must wait until we have finished estimating the pricing block in our model, the evidence from other econometric studies (including the empirical work which has been carried out in connection with the best known Keynesian models) would suggest that the secular rate of inflation can be better explained by the growth of money wages in excess of labor productivity, together with other factors affecting the unit costs of production, than by the growth of the money stock. Indeed, the empirical work which has already been done in connection with our own model would suggest that, if an attempt is made to control the growth of the money stock in the mistaken view that it (or the monetary base) is an exogenously determined policy variable, the result will be not so much a slowdown in the rate of inflation (except to the extent the Phillips curve applies) as a decline in the level of real economic activity. From this perspective, the Fed's nonaccommodating policy which monetarists advocate is simply another means of trying to limit the growth of money wages, in this case through a higher unemployment rate and depressed commodity markets rather than some other, less self-destructive form of incomes policy.

Notes

1. No matter what additional variables were included in the estimating equation, or how the equation was specified (e.g., first differences, growth rates, etc.), it proved impossible to obtain an R^2 greater than zero when regressing the change in the commercial banking system's nonborrowed reserves against the change in the Federal Reserve System's holdings of government securities, using the quarterly data available for the period between 1952 and 1978.

2. This alternative approach can be traced back to Guttentag, 1966; Hendershott, 1968; and Lombra and Torto, 1973. Indeed, it was the Lombra and Torto article which first enabled us to understand the lack of direct correlation between the Fed's open-market operations and bank reserves (see note 1 above). See also Lombra (1981) and Lombra and Kaufman (1982) for the most recent work along these same lines.

3. Until recently, under the system of delayed reserve accounting, commercial banks had two weeks after the close of the period to obtain any additional reserves they needed to meet their legal requirements. Under the changes recently announced, they will need to maintain reserves equal to some average of their liabilities over a preceding two-week period.

4. Only certain of the items from the Fed's balance sheet were found to be correlated with the change in its holdings of government securities. These were 1.) the amount of float; 2.) the gold stock (in the earlier part of the period covered, before gold sales were terminated); 3.) Treasury currency outstanding; and 4.) Treasury deposits at the Fed. As for the other six items, see below, note 5.

5. An effort has been made to identify the size of the error factor by equating it with any change in the other six items from the Fed's balance sheet which were found not to be predictors of a change in the Fed's holdings of government securities (see above, note 4). This approach,

however, understates the error factor, since it makes no allowance for the possibility that the Fed incorrectly anticipated a change in the other variables included in equation 5. For a more complete discussion, see Forman, Groves and Eichner, 1983.

6. Again, this explained more fully in Forman, Groves and Eichner, 1983.

7. Except for the ratio of free to total reserves, the variables have all been detrended by calculating, for each quarterly observation, the deviation from some central tendency, whether it be the exponential growth rate, as in the case of *Dep*, *DD*, and *M1*, or the linear growth trend, as in the case of *L* and the federal funds rate itself. For a further discussion of this technique for minimizing the effect of any serial correlation, see Forman and Eichner, 1981.

8. While it might appear that the explanatory power of equation 6 could be increased by adding *M1* as an additional independent variable (see equation 9), the slight increase in the value of the *R2* statistic from 0.80 to 0.82 is only because of the collinearity between *M1* and *L* and between *M1* and *ResF*/*ResT*. The collinearity is evident from the way the coefficients change when *M1* is added to equation 6 and by the correlation coefficient of 0.53, which has been calculated for *L* and *M1* (compared with a correlation coefficient of −0.16 for *L* and *ResF*/*ResT* and a correlation coefficient of −0.21 for *ResF*/*ResT* and *M1*). *M1* would thus appear to have no independent explanatory power of its own (see equation 5). The statistically significant relationship which is often observed between *M1* and various short-term interest rates, such as the federal funds rate, instead reflects the degree of liquidity pressure within the commercial banking system, *L*, and the ratio of free to total reserves, *ResF*/*ResT*, with which *M1* is correlated. *L*, *ResF*/*ResT*, and *M1* all vary together over time because all three depend on how accommodating the Fed's open-market operations are. However, while the degree of liquidity pressure and the ratio of free to total reserves each exert an independent influence on the federal funds rate, the same is not true of *M1*, which appears to have explanatory power only because it is so highly collinear with *L*.

The outcome of using *Dep* or *DD* in place of *M1* produces results which are only slightly different.

References

Cooley, T. F. and LeRoy, S. F. 1981. Identification and Estimation of Money Demand. *American Economic Review*, December.

Judd, J. P. and Scadding, J. L. 1982. The Search for a Stable Money Demand Function: A Survey of the Post-1973 Literature. *Journal of Economic Literature*, September.

Eichner, A. S. 1977. The Geometry of Macrodynamic Balance. *Australian Economic Papers*, June.

Eichner, A. S. 1979. A Post-Keynesian Short-Period Model. *Journal of Post-Keynesian Economics*, Summer.

Forman, L. and Eichner, A. S. 1981. A Post-Keynesian Short-Period Model: Some Preliminary Econometric Results. *Journal of Post-Keynesian Economics*, Autumn.

Forman, L., Groves, M., and Eichner, A. S. 1983. The Monetary-Financial Block of a Post-Keynesian Short-Period Model. CEAR working paper, no. 5 (revised), unpublished, September.

Guttentag, J. 1966. The Strategy of Open Market Operations. *Quarterly Journal of Economics*, February.

Hendershott, P. 1968. *The Neutralized Money Stock: An Unbiased Measure of Federal Reserve Actions*. Homewood, IL, Irwin.

Lombra, R. E. 1981. Financial Innovation, Deregulation and the Effectiveness of Monetary Policy: A Graphical Approach. Unpublished.

Lombra, R. E. and Torto, R. G. 1973. Federal Reserve 'Defensive' Behavior and the Reverse Causation Argument. *Southern Economic Journal*, July.

Lombra, R. E. and Kaufman, H. M. 1982. The Money Supply Process: Stability and Simultaneity. Unpublished.

Minsky, H. P. 1982. *Can 'It' Happen Again*? Armonk, N.Y., M. E. Sharpe.

3 FINANCIAL INNOVATION AND CONTROL OF THE MONEY SUPPLY: *The Radcliffe Report Revisited*

Stephen Rousseas

Apart from Monetarism, the two major postwar attempts to redefine monetary policy were the United States availability of credit doctrine in 1951 and the Radcliffe committee report of 1959. Although substantively different, there was a common core running through both of them and, in the end, the Radcliffe committee, in a monumental failure of nerve, embraced one of the main tenets of the availability of credit doctrine—the locking-in effect. In view of the current monetary turmoil in the United States and Britain and the revived interest in the Radcliffe liquidity thesis as a basis for a theory of money-supply endogeneity, it might be worthwhile to have another look.

1. The Availability of Credit Doctrine

The availability of credit doctrine was the product of Robert V. Roosa (1951) and Allan Sproul (1951), who were respectively vice president and president of the Federal Reserve Bank of New York. It was a doctrine generated within the Federal Reserve System to justify the March 1951 Treasury-Federal Reserve accord that freed the Federal Reserve from the wartime dominance of the Treasury. Its purpose was to assuage any fear that a return to an active monetary policy would engender high interest rates and a collapse of the economy. After the lively and at times acrimonious debate leading to the accord, some assurances had to be given. In a sense, 1951, the date of the accord, can be taken as the date upon which the dominance of Keynesian fiscal policy over monetary policy began its descent, leading to the ultimate triumph of Monetarism in the 1980s and the rout of Keynesian economics.

Traditional reliance on open-market operations involved changes in the interest rate over a relatively large range. The effectiveness of monetary policy was therefore based on viewing the interest rate as a cost to the borrower, i.e., in curtailing the demand for money and credit. With the rising profit expectations of an upswing, large increases in interest rates would be required to contain the inflationary upsurge. At a time when the Keynesian paradigm reigned virtually unchallenged, a monetary policy based on high interest rates was seen to be fraught with danger; it threatened to bludgeon the economy into a decline. It was in response to this fear that the supporters of monetary policy came up with an ingenious theory that fed into the political sensibilities of the time by arguing that monetary policy now had the delicacy of a precision tool—it could do the job within a very narrow range of interest-rate variation.

The principal argument was one of increased sensitivity, which emphasized the impact of small changes in interest rates on the expectations of investors. For example, Robert V. Roosa wrote that "the desired degree of tightness can no doubt be obtained with a relatively small price (rate) change—so small, perhaps, as superficially to appear trivial. But the potency of such a change comes from the impact of 'uncertainty' upon markets dominated by sensitive investors" (1951, p. 284). In a similar vein, Allan Sproul wrote that "the money market . . . is still sensitive (and will continue to be sensitive) to relatively small changes in the interest rate structure and to any uncertainty concerning the future direction of such changes, in terms of its readiness to make funds available for expansion" (1951, p. 322). Carried away by his enthusiasm for the new doctrine, Richard Musgrave pulled out all the stops. "Let us suppose now," he wrote, "that the government does not actually increase the supply of debt or reduce the supply of reserve money, but merely leads investors to believe that such steps will be taken . . . Indeed, *the creation of expectations that rates will rise by x points will do more to tighten the market than will an actual rise by x points*" (1951, pp. 235–36, italics supplied).

It was the enormous increase of the gross federal debt held by the public, from $43 billion in 1940 to $242 billion at the end of the war in 1946, that now made it possible to use open-market operations for finely controlling the overall liquidity of the economy. The public debt, moreover, resulted in a markedly more integrated and interrelated credit market which guaranteed the rapid transmission of monetary policy to all sectors of that market. Not only banks, but all nonbank financial intermediaries would be equally affected. Implicit in the argument was the assumption that the underlying financial structure would remain unchanged and that small interest-rate changes would "lock in" the holders of the public debt, preventing, in the face of potential capital losses, both borrowers and lenders from converting their earning assets into cash for the financing of their various projects.

The availability of credit doctrine shifted the argument from the demand to the supply side. It was the availability of credit, not the interest rate as a cost to borrowers, that was paramount. The interest rate, in other words, was now a proxy for the supply-side effects of open-market operations. Moreover, the volume of open-market operations would be sharply reduced because of the size of the public debt. The reason for this newfound effectiveness of open-market operations was the existence of nonbank financial intermediaries (NFIs) who were also bloated with government securities in the immediate postwar period. The ultraconservative portfolio managers of NFIs were seen to have a strong aversion to the potential capital losses that small interest-rate changes would bring about. Therefore, a very small interest-rate change would lock them into government securities and prevent an increase in the supply of credit via a conversion from government securities to other more profitable loans.

The locking-in effect, however, proved to be a mirage. The shorter the maturity, the weaker the locking-in effect would be (Smith, 1956). Or, to put it otherwise, the greater the interest rate increase would have to be in order to lock them in—which, of course, undercut the very basis upon which the availability of credit doctrine was founded, especially in view of the low average maturity of the public debt. The banks in particular, as the greatest suppliers of credit, were flooded with Treasury bills (TBs), the shortest of all maturities. All the banks had to do to withstand the pressures of the tight-money policies of the central bank was to refuse the frequent rollovers of maturing TBs. And even when, in the 1960s, the banks had worked off their holding of TBs, certificates of deposits (CDs) and Eurodollars came rushing on the scene as offsets to the central bank's monetary policy. Not surprisingly, the income velocity of money moved sharply up and along a given $V(i)$-curve—as any good Keynesian would have expected—via the activation of idle balances and the economizing of transactions balances. In addition, the velocity curve shifted outwards as a result of new financial innovations that made a mockery of the putative effectiveness of monetary policy under the availability of credit doctrine.

Apart from the impact of open-market operations on potential lenders via the locking-in effect, the availability of credit doctrine also argued that changes in the interest rate would also have a direct effect on borrowers via a wealth effect. Even within the narrower range of variation, an increase in interest rates would cause bond prices to fall, thus causing a drop in the value of existing portfolios and the net worth of individuals holding them. The demand for credit would therefore fall as well as the level of expenditures because of the drop in liquidity. Indeed, the drop in liquidity caused by moderately higher interest rates would cause an increase in the demand for cash and for prime risk-free near-monies, such as government securities. The net result would be a fall in the supply of loanable funds as well as a drop in the demand for them (Lindbeck, 1962). These wealth effects, however, were secondary to the locking-in effect itself. Next down the scale of importance were the arguments concerning credit standards and credit rationing. With the locking-in effect firmly in place on the supply side and the availability of credit greatly reduced as a result of a disproportionately small increase in interest rates, credit standards would rise dramatically, leading to what Keynes called in the *Treatise* "a fringe of unsatisfied borrowers."

The availability of credit doctrine was not tested until the expansion of 1955–1957, four years after the accord—and it foundered. The locking-in effect turned out to be wishful thinking in support of an idea that had its origins in a political struggle to reinstate monetary policy in the immediate aftermath of World War II. Short-term interest rates more than doubled and velocity rose by 14 percent. It was out of this failure of the availability of credit doctrine that the monetarist dogma came into its own in the 1960s and culminated in the October 1979 decision of Paul Volcker to give up any attempt to influence interest rates directly. Open-market operations were now to be used to keep a series of monetary aggregates within certain specified targets in keeping with monetarist principles. Interest rates would be free to seek their own market-determined levels unhindered by the central bank—as indeed they did with the prime rate soaring above 20 percent. Keynesians were in full rout, but before that ultimate monetarist takeover, one other serious attempt was made to redefine monetary policy in the 1950s.

2. The Radcliffe Liquidity Thesis

At virtually the same time as the United States availability of credit doctrine was heralding the newfound virility of monetary policy, a new thesis was being propounded in Britain by a specially appointed commission that severely undercut the United States position. After two years of hearings and written submissions of evidence from a wide spectrum covering the banking, government, business, and academic communities, the Radcliffe committee issued its report on *The Working of the Monetary System* (1959). It forms the basis for the modern post-Keynesian view of the endogeneity of the money supply—although, in the end, the Radcliffe committee, traumatized by its findings, had a failure of nerve and embraced one of the major arguments of the American availability of credit doctrine. The report cast serious doubt on the effectiveness of monetary policy within the neoclassical synthesis of "Keynesianism without tears." It was before its time and it reaped the hostility of those unwilling to give up on the notion of the money supply as the key exogenous variable in monetary policy. Indeed, the major conclusions of the report implied, and some of its expert witnesses stated openly, that an uncritical reliance on conventional monetary policy could well undermine and undo the objectives of fiscal policy—as in fact turned out to be the case in the events that followed.

The main concern of the Radcliffe committee was to discover how recent changes in the underlying structure "had modified the ability of the authorities to influence the [economic] system by monetary methods" (Report 1959, p. 3). For any meaningful evaluation of monetary policy, changes in the structure of financial institutions had to be taken into account as they occurred over historical time. Their overall conclusion was that the money supply had become largely irrelevant and that an effective monetary policy could only be achieved by control over the general liquidity of the economy.

The members of the Radcliffe committee were concerned, as were their availability counterparts in the United States, with the damage that high interest rates might do to the economy. Toward the end of the 1950s, largely as a result of the forced savings during the war and the widely held wartime public debt, the British economy, like that of the United States, was "oozing surplus liquidity," and any attempt to offset it by traditional open-market operations would require dangerously high interest rates to stifle the obvious intentions of consumers, producers, and merchants to divest themselves of this surplus (1959, p. 15). The unequal directional effects of traditional monetary policy, moreover, caused severe distortions in the channels of economic activity, in the view of the Radcliffe committee, and threatened the pace of investment and technological innovation through high interest-rate policies.

The Radcliffe liquidity thesis, therefore, led to the rejection of traditional monetary policy and its dependence on what the committee called *the interest-incentive effect*, or the attempt of the monetary authorities to influence the level of aggregate demand through the impact of interest-rate changes on investment. "We have sought, without much success," wrote the committee about the interest-incentive effect within its normal range, "for convincing evidence of its presence in recent years" (1959, p. 131).[1] The committee then turned to its major finding, the general liquidity effect: "[T]he monetary authorities can bring about a change in the liquidity condition of financial institutions and of business firms and people generally, so that those wanting money to spend (whether for capital development or other purposes) find it more (or less) difficult to get than before" (1959, pp. 130–31). Here the Radcliffe report veered toward the United States availability of credit doctrine, though no explicit reference is made to it. If the interest-rate effect on the demand side, within its institutionally feasible range, can be swamped by the profit expectations of businessmen, the only way to abort the demand for money is through severe restrictions on the availability of credit. As the committee noted, "[I]f the money for financing the project cannot be got on any tolerable terms at all, *that is the end of the matter*" (1959, p. 131, italics supplied). But restricting the availability of credit implies more than just restricting the money supply, which is only a part of the general liquidity of the economy. "It is the whole liquidity position that is relevant to spending decisions," not just the money supply, for "decisions to spend on goods and services—the decisions that determine the level of demand—are influenced by the liquidity of spenders" as well as by "the liquidity of the various groups of financial institutions" (1959, p. 132). In other words, account must be taken not only of the income, the convertible assets, and the borrowing power of spenders, but also of "the methods, moods and resources of financial institutions and other firms which are prepared (on terms) to finance other people's spending" (1959, p. 132). The Radcliffe committee then went on to hammer home its point on the irrelevance of the money supply as the object of monetary control: "[S]pending is not limited by the amount of money in existence; . . . it is related to the amount of money people think they can get hold of, whether by receipts of income (for instance from sales), by disposal of capital assets or by borrowing. . . . *[S]pending is not limited by the amount of money in existence [as can be seen] by reference to the velocity of circulation*" (1959, p. 133, italics supplied).

If the conventional money supply is restricted or held constant and the level of spending, nevertheless, continues to increase—as it is wont to do—this can only mean that the velocity of circulation has gone up. Within traditional monetary theory, of the Keynesian variety, there is supposed to be some outer limit to velocity, for when all idle balances have been activated and transactions balances have been pared to the bone in response to excessively high interest rates, then velocity will have reached its theoretical maximum and nominal GNP would have to grind to a halt—at which point conventional monetary policy would hold. This, of course, assumes a stable financial framework which, in turn, implies the total absence of financial innovations. Apart from the problem of closing the barn door after the horse is gone, the existence of a velocity maximum can itself be challenged, as indeed the Radcliffe committee did. "[W]e cannot find," wrote the Committee, "any reason for supposing, or any experience in monetary history indicating, that there is any limit to the velocity of circulation of money" (1959, p. 133). This was the most important statement in the entire report, the full implications of which the committee failed to grasp.

Trapped within its own traditional way of looking at the demand for money, the committee was reluctant to make "more use of this concept" on the grounds that velocity "is a statistical concept that tells us nothing of the motivation that influences the level of demand. An analysis of liquidity, on the other hand, directs attention to the behaviour and decisions that do directly influence the level of demand" (1959, p. 133). The committee, in effect, chose to remain within the Cambridge tradition which emphasizes k over V. The difference is between "money sitting" and "money on the wing." The Cambridge tradition prefers "money sitting," because it leads directly to the psychological motives for holding money—with its emphasis on the demand for money—as compared to the mechanical barreling of the money supply through the economy in the form of Irving Fisher's V. Although *liquidity*, as used by the committee, is identical to *velocity*, the committee's failure to follow up on the explicit use of V was unfortunate, since the concept of velocity focuses attention more directly on the impact of financial innovations—a more important phenomenon on the supply side (which turned out to be the committee's main concern in the report) than the demand-side motives for holding money. Events subsequent to the report make it even more important to return to the concept of velocity, especially in the current situation.

If a velocity maximum is the outer limit of a movement along an increasingly steep $V(i)$-function, then the absence of such a maximum must imply a series of parametric shifts of the $V(i)$-curve to the right—which is another way of talking about the impact of financial innovations on the effective money supply, now without any upper limit to itself or to the nominal GNP. In these terms, the shambles of conventional monetary policy becomes transparent.[2] From the Radcliffe committee's point of view, emphasis was therefore to be placed "on all those groups of institutions whose behaviour seems to bear in an important degree on the amount of liquidity, rather than just the amount of money, in the economy" (1959, p. 133). Financial innovations and control over the velocity changes they induce are the critical factor for any effective monetary policy—one that goes considerably beyond an attempt to control the credit-creating function of the commercial banking system. It was clear to the Radcliffe committee that "the more efficient the financial structure, the more can the velocity of circulation be stretched without serious inconvenience being caused" (1959, p. 133). The door was wide open for selective credit controls over a wide range of financial institutions, but the Radcliffe committee slammed the door shut and took refuge in its own version of the locking-in effect. Before going into this, however, the *Memoranda of Evidence* (Volume 3, Part XIII, 1959) should be brought in.

3. Memoranda of Evidence

Most, if not all, the economists who gave testimony rejected the idea that a predominant emphasis on monetary policy could achieve stability at full employment. At best, monetary policy could only support fiscal policy in a subordinate capacity. Yet key contributors to the *Memoranda*, in 1959, even rejected the notion that an optimum combination of monetary and fiscal policy would work. The artificial restoration of Say's law through "the skillful use of fiscal and monetary policy" could not succeed in forcing the economy "into behaving like a neoclassical model" (Samuelson, 1964). Variations in the rate of interest through open-market operations were powerless to serve as the regulator of the economy within the confines of the neoclassical synthesis.

The strongest argument came from A. J. Brown (*Memoranda*, 1959). Given that prices are a mark-up over unit prime costs and the degree of monopoly in the economy is relatively stable, then variations in profit margins are due to variations in the level of economic activity (capacity utilization). Insofar as traditional monetary policy has little, if any direct effect on prime costs, its principal effect will not be on prices but on the level of output and hence on profits. If carried to an extreme, monetary policy can, of course, lower the rate of inflation but only by raising the unemployment rate to record levels—as was the case, during the early 1980s, in Britain under Margaret Thatcher and in the United States under Ronald Reagan. In the words of Brown, "In an industrial economy the compression of profit margins does not seem to be a very promising field for attack on price inflation by monetary policy. The immediate effect is likely to reduce production (probably with increased total cost-per-unit) rather than price reduction" (*Memoranda*, p. 49). For Brown, the cost of labor is the main determinant of prices. The real costs of an effective monetary policy are therefore to be found in the serious underemployment of labor and equipment (as a means for breaking the power of trade unions) and in the slowing down of the rate of technological innovation.

R. F. Kahn was equally forceful in stating the case: "It is the rise in wages which is the cause of prices rising. . . . The normal situation is . . . one in which the behaviour of prices is determined by the course of wage negotiations, so that any progressive rise in prices is a 'cost inflation' . . . If reliance is placed on regulation of demand in order to secure a tolerable behaviour of prices, it must certainly mean maintaining unemployment at a level which would represent very serious economic waste. . . . The economic waste involved in such a policy is particularly great if demand is regulated by restricting productive investment, as will be the main result of relying on monetary policy" (*Memoranda*, 1959, p. 142). The solution to the problem of maintaining a stable price level is not to be found in monetary policy, but "in the realm of wage negotiation." In short, an incomes policy is a prerequisite for price stability. To attempt to achieve it through monetary policy would end in perverse results.

The Radcliffe committee, however, did not mention the arguments of Brown and Kahn, choosing instead to emphasize its liquidity thesis of limitless velocity changes. Nicholas Kaldor came the closest in approaching the main concerns of the committee. He flatly denied any direct relationship between the money supply and the level of nominal income. "To proceed from one to the other," he argued, "it is necessary to postulate that changes in the supply of money leave the frequency with which money changes hands (the so-called "velocity of circulation") unaffected" (*Memoranda*, 1959, p. 146)—and, he could have added, the pace of financial innovations in the economy. Kaldor, however, seemed to restrict himself more to movements along the $V(i)$-curve than to its shifts, thus playing down the role of financial innovations in the "spectacular rise in the velocity of circulation." His emphasis in explaining changes in velocity was the conventional Keynesian one of the activation of idle balances and the economizing of transactions balances (p. 147). Kaldor was, nevertheless, clear on the limitations of monetary policy: "[T]he *impact* effect of any change in the money supply is not on the level of payments at all, but on the velocity of circulation" (p. 146, original italics). Kaldor went on to agree with Brown and Kahn that monetary policy is effective only in extremis, i.e., by such "drastic steps in raising interest rates" that unemployment would increase to unprecedented postwar levels, and the functioning of capital and credit markets would be destabilized. In the end, Kaldor came out on the side of Brown and Kahn: "[W]hen the driving force behind inflation is an excessive rate of increase in money wages . . . [the problem of controlling] wage inflation . . . is not one that can be expected to be cured by restrictions of demand—not unless the restriction is carried to the point of such heavy unemployment that the wage earners in any particular industry are unable to hold out for higher wages" (p. 150). Clearly, an effective and permanent incomes policy is needed. I. M. D. Little, R. R. Neild, and C. R. Ross argued along similar lines (*Memoranda*, 1959, pp. 159–67).

Although all the makings of what is now called post-Keynesian economics were in place in the 1959 *Memoranda of Evidence*, the Radcliffe committee chose to ignore them and limited itself, instead, to grappling with the monster it had let loose in the form of the liquidity thesis.

4. The Committee's Failure of Nerve

Having to face what it had unleashed, the Radcliffe committee took refuge in its own version of the locking-in effect: "[A] movement of rates of interest, quite apart from any direct effect it may have on the demand for investment [which the committee thought was little enough] may have appreciable effects on the behaviour of various financial institutions. . . . Provided that it is not confined to the short end of the market, *a movement of interest rates implies significant changes in the capital value of many assets held by financial institutions*" (*Report*, 1959, p. 133, italics supplied).

The balance sheet, or wealth effects, of interest-rate policy was brought into full play as a counterbalance to the committee's dismissal of the interest-incentive effect, on the demand side, as a cost to borrowers. For the committee, this was "an important conclusion for policy" since it implied "that movements in interest rates have an effect apart from any influence they have on the incentive to hold capital goods" (p. 134)—the latter being, of course, minimal within the prevailing range of interest rate variation extant at that time.

Mimicking their United States availability of credit counterparts, the Radcliffe committee had shifted to the supply side with its emphasis on playing the full maturity spectrum of government securities. Given the locking-in effect, which is nowhere referred to as such in the report, it is the "structure of interest rates rather than some notion of the 'supply of money' . . . [which becomes] the centre-piece of monetary action" (p. 18). Properly handled, the general liquidity problem could be met on the supply side by restrictions on the availability of credit. Interest rates, as in "bastard" Keynesian theory, were to be the key to a proper use of monetary policy, but not via the *IS-LM* analysis of the neoclassical synthesis. It would now be predominantly the supply-side effects of interest rate changes over the full maturity spectrum of government securities that would do the trick. Their impact on the capital values of financial institutions would now transform monetary policy into the effective tool it had never been before.

Having dethroned the money supply and having replaced it with the principle of general liquidity, the committee quickly took flight from the implications of its position and retreated back into a manipulation of the interest-rate structure. It could have learned a lesson by studying the demise of the United States American availability of credit doctrine in 1955–1957. Interestingly enough, no Americans were asked to testify before the committee.

In reflecting on its own general liquidity thesis, however, the committee became uncomfortable with what it had wrought and readily acknowledged the negative implications of its own novel approach to monetary policy: "[I]f we are right in believing that the level of total demand is influenced by the lending behaviour of an infinitely wide range of financial institutions, and not just the supply of money, it might be supposed that we should substitute for the traditional control of the money supply a complex of controls over that wide range of financial institutions. Such a prospect would be unwelcome *except as a last resort*, not mainly because of its administrative burdens, but because the further growth of new financial institutions would allow the situation continually to slip from the grip of the authorities" (p. 134, italics supplied). The committee then went on to reassure itself: "The fact that operations on the structure of interest rates do, for institutional reasons, change the liquidity of financial operators throughout the economy should make it possible to avoid any such complex of direct controls" (p. 134).

Reliance on nonmonetary measures and resort to "a comprehensive structure of financial controls" became admissible only in desperate straights—or, it could be added, if the locking-in effect does not work, which it does not from all the experience we have had with the use of monetary policy to drive up interest rates from (in the United States) 1955 to the present. If the locking-in effect indeed does not work and financial innovations are rampant (both of which are true on the current American scene) then, on the Radcliffe committee's own terms, there is no other recourse than to "a complex system of controls"—the very thing the

Committee wished to avoid "except as a last resort." The Committee had a clear failure of nerve. It failed to face up to the issue of a runaway income velocity of money and the need to address that issue in terms of direct monetary controls.

5. Selective Credit Controls

On the issue of direct controls, the Radcliffe committee could have profited by paying more attention to the submitted testimony it published in its *Memoranda*. "The problem," for Thomas Balogh, was "whether central bank policy can . . . be made more effective . . . without varying the rate of interest, through direct control of the volume of bank credit and forcing, in the ultimate analysis, credit rationing on the banks without moral suasion and appeals" (p. 35). For R. F. Kahn, "[M]onetary controls provide a very unreliable and clumsy method of regulating investment. Some differentiation of rates should be possible as between one industry and another and one type of investment and another" (p. 146). Even for Harry Johnson (in his 1959 pre-monetarist phase) "[T]he use of Bank rate to initiate changes in monetary policy, and open-market operations in bills to make the Bank rate effective, is unnecessarily costly and inefficient. . . . [M]any types of credit transactions which are most likely to cause trouble are more expeditiously tackled by specific methods such as capital issues control, bank advance directives, and hire-purchase restrictions" (p. 137).

Of special interest is the position of R. S. Sayers, one of the key members of the Radcliffe committee. The sixth edition of his book, *Modern Banking* (1964), incorporated some of the major findings of the committee. Sayers, however, did not pick up on the issue of selective controls, limiting himself instead to what can best be called moral suasion with a stick, or the threat of selective controls to induce compliance. It is not a very convincing argument, and certainly not one to be applied to the U.S. monetary system with its 14,000 banks compared to Britain's handful, but at least by 1964 Sayers had retreated from the locking-in effect of the Radcliffe committee. Sayers did recognize, however, that the "choice is between an emphasis on raising interest rates and on direct interference with banks and other financial intermediaries by raising liquidity ratio requirements and/or direct restraints on lending." Since the "interest-incentive effect is slow to operate," the choice for Sayers was "*between administrative cumbersomeness on the one hand and inequity and inefficiency on the other*" (1964, p. 257, italics supplied).

The need for selective monetary controls stems directly from the ineffectiveness of traditional monetary policy—its "inequity and inefficiency"—particularly as a result of financial innovations. It is the elasticity of the credit structure that has become the problem, much of it in response to the monetarist targeting of all-elusive monetary aggregates with interest rates set free to find their market levels. Monetary policy has become an exercise in futility. *Nous pedalons dans la choucroute*, as French wit would put it. In Radcliffe terms, the liquidity structure has been transformed by the radically changing complex of financial claims to such an extent that there no longer is any direct relationship between it and the long-term growth of the economy, with banks now "playing a relatively smaller part than before." In the words of R. S. Sayers, "There is no fixed barrier between what is and what is not banking, and how important banks are, and how important are other financial intermediaries, depends upon the extent to which innovation of financial devices is shared by banks or is left to the ingenuity of financiers outside the banks" (1964, p. 174).

6. Conclusion

Traditional monetary policy, with its fixation on the money supply as an exogenous entity (whether based on "bastard" Keynesian or monetarist theory), is clearly inadequate and, more recently, perverse in its effects. Its postwar record warrants the conclusion. Modern monetary policy and the active use of open-market operations dates, for the United States at least, from 1955 or four years after the Treasury-Federal Reserve accord. It has been around, in other words, for less than 30 years, and in that brief time, it has been buffeted by a series of theories—from the availability of credit doctrine (and its Radcliffe counterpart), to the bills-only policy, to the fine-tuning of neoclassical Keynesianism, to the rules of Monetarism—none of which has worked for the obvious reason that all regard the money supply as exogenous and therefore subject to indirect central-bank control.

What is needed is a return to the major concern of Keynes in his *Tract on Monetary Reform*—the offsetting and control of changes in velocity—with full recognition of the endogenous nature of the money supply. As endogenous as the money supply may be, however, it does not mean that accommodation to the "needs of trade" takes place smoothly or equitably or that it is without cost in terms of distortions in the flow of credit. The problem of controlling the paths it takes by controlling the flow of credit through the economy remains—a problem most post-Keynesian monetary theorists have ignored. Post-Keynesian theory must therefore move in the direction of combining selective credit controls with a permanent incomes policy. Not only must wages be controlled, but the flow of credit as well.

Post-Keynesian economics can avoid degenerating to the tinkering of mechanical solutions only by facing up to the need for coordinating economic policy. In short, it must move in the direction of economic planning within a capitalist system that entails a social contract for the distribution of income—to be worked out jointly by capital, labor, and government. It also requires the "socialization of investment" that Keynes discussed toward the end of his *General Theory*. The direct socialization of investment, however, need not imply massive amounts of state investment. The same effect could be achieved through direct and selective controls over the flow of credit in the economy.

The combination of incomes policy with selective credit controls is not meant as a cure-all for the ills and troubles of a capitalist society. The path of capitalism through historical time will continue to be troubled and its survival in the very long run cannot be assured. The need for a willful coordination of economic policy is a recognition that the allocation of resources through an impersonal market system is nothing more than the stuff and mythology of economic textbooks. The unavoidable alternative is the discretionary application of human intelligence to the solution of social problems. If a permanent incomes policy and a system of selective credit controls prove to be politically impossible, either singly or in combination, then *that* is the problem of capitalism.

Notes

1. Substantial support for the committee's finding is to be found in the *Memoranda of Evidence* (Vol. 3, Part XIII, 1959). This finding, however, holds for the institutionally feasible range of interest rate variation; that is, between the interest-rate floor and a conventionally held interest-rate ceiling. Given this relatively narrow range in the recent past, interest rate considerations (as a cost to borrowers) could be easily swamped by the profit expectations of business during boom periods. It is only with the October 1979 policy shift of Paul Volcker in the United States, and its equivalent in Britain under the Thatcher government, that interest rates have been uncapped. In these new circumstances, the extraordinary level of interest rates, acting on the demand side, would seem to have given a new life to the interest rate as a cost to borrowers.

2. For two early expositions of this argument, see Minsky, Central Banking and Money Market Changes, reprinted in Minsky, H. P. 1982. *Can "It" Happen Again*?, New York, M. E. Sharpe; and Rousseas, S. W. 1960. Velocity Changes and the Effectiveness of Monetary Policy, 1951–1957, *Review of Economics and Statistics*, February. For a more recent and surprising discussion of the problem of financial innovation from the current president of the

Federal Reserve Bank of New York, see Solomon, A. M. 1982. *Financial Innovation and Monetary Policy, Federal Reserve Bank of New York.*

References

Committee on the Working of the Monetary System: Principal Memoranda of Evidence, Vol. 3, Part XIII. 1959. London, HMSO.

Committee on the Working of the Monetary System: Report. 1959. London, HMSO.

Lindbeck, A. 1962. *The "New" Theory of Credit in the United States*. 2nd ed. Stockholm, Almqvist & Wicksell.

Musgrave, R. A. 1951. Money, Liquidity and the Valuation of Assets. In: *Money, Trade, and Economic Growth: In Honor of J. H. Williams*, New York, Macmillan.

Roosa, R. V. 1951. Interest Rates and the Central Bank. In: *Money, Trade, and Economic Growth: In Honor of J. H. Williams*, New York, Macmillan.

Samuelson, P. A. 1964. The General Theory. In: Lekachman, R., ed., *Keynes's General Theory: Reports of Three Decades*, New York, St. Martin's Press.

Sayers, R. S. 1964. *Modern Banking*, 6th ed. London, Oxford University Press.

Smith, W. L. 1956. On the Effectiveness of Monetary Policy. *American Economic Review*, September.

Sproul, A. 1951. Changing Concepts of Central Banking. In: *Money, Trade, and Economic Growth: In Honor of J. H. Williams*, New York, Macmillan.

4 CREDIT AND MONEY: *The Dynamic Circuit, Overdraft Economics, and Post-Keynesian Economics*

Marc Lavoie

1. Keynes, Nobel Prizes, and Nonorthodox Currents in Monetary Economics

There are two dangers when starting to study money matters. One is to follow Keynes too closely, in particular his writings in the *General Theory* (1936). The other danger is to look to the writings of Nobel laureates on monetary issues. To acquire a clear and proper understanding of the true functioning of production money economies, one should keep clear of these authors.

Against Keynes and his *General Theory*, much has been said, both from those who want to reconstruct Walrasian economics and from those who want to demolish it (Bharadwaj, 1983, p. 4). Unfortunately, most students of economics never read Keynes. Those who have, however, have generally highly benefited from Keynes' difficulties in escaping from old ideas and the

---

This article followed several discussions with Professors Sheila Dow (Stirling University, Scotland) and Alain Parguez (Université de Besançon, France). Of course they do not and cannot be assumed to agree with every statement made by the author. As a matter of fact, none of the authors quoted in the text may be assumed to be in agreement with the interpretations put forward in the text. I would also want to thank my teammate, Eli Sukunda, for his help.

somewhat ambiguous and mysterious character of the *General Theory* (Kurz, 1983, p. 42). To understand economics it is not enough to ask, as Jacques Henry (1982, p. 19) points out, "What did Maynard really say," or "What did Maynard mean to say," or finally, "What did Maynard think he was really saying." One must remember that in writing the *General Theory*, Keynes faced two hurdles: he had trouble breaking away from tradition, but also had to keep within tradition to make himself understood. There are severe limitations to the *General Theory*. They are due, "not to any basic defect in those aspects that were fundamentally new", but to the failure of Keynes "to escape from traditional modes of thought" (Kaldor 1983, p. 3). It is therefore important to go beyond Keynes, in particular on monetary matters, and to search for *trans-Keynesian* principles (Parguez 1983, p. 4) which transcends Keynes' break from neoclassical economics and which are better adapted to the description and the analysis of modern economies.

In speaking against Nobel laureates, I have four of them in mind: Friedrich von Hayek, Milton Friedman, James Tobin and Paul Samuelson. Hayek's model of a credit economy (in *Prices and Production* (1967) and in later works) was identified from the onset by Piero Sraffa (1932) as an utopian non-monetary economy, from which debts, money-contracts or wage settlements were absent.[1] Friedman pretends that the proper methodology to study positive monetary economics is to assume that money falls from the sky, thrown out of a helicopter by the gnomes of the Federal Reserve System (1969, p. 4). Such assumptions can only seem reasonable to other Nobel laureates, such as those who postulate the existence of futures markets stretching into infinity.[2]

Students of money economics must also be wary of those responsible for the so-called neoclassical synthesis. As argued recently from both critical sides of the Keynesian orthodoxy (Lucas 1981; Minsky 1981), Tobin's present economics are a slightly modified version of 1970's Friedmanian economics.[3] As to Paul Samuelson, although he has not directly intervened in the debates on money, he has put some of his opinions in print, for instance:

> "[There] still do exist in England men whose minds were formed in 1939, and who haven't changed a thought since that time, and who . . . say money doesn't matter. They've embalmed their views in the Radcliffe Committee, one of the most sterile operations of all time" (Samuelson, 1969, p. 7).[4]

In this article, I will endeavor to show that Samuelson's comments are mistaken. Those British economists who influenced the Radcliffe committee in the late 1950s do have a very clear understanding of the role and the importance of money and credit in a modern production economy. In fact, I will show that the views of these economists, which I call Cambridge post-Keynesians, are supported by a wide range of currents in monetary thought.

For exposition purposes I will classify these currents under four headings: the Cambridge post-Keynesians, the American post-Keynesians, the economists of overdraft economies, and the economists of the dynamic circuit. In the remainder of the article, I will synthesize their common theses on monetary phenomena, and I will attempt to explain their divergences. But before doing so, I think some definition of the four identified groups is in order.

The Cambridge post-Keynesians include those economists who have assigned themselves the task of perpetuating the Keynesian revolution, in particular in the field of capital and distribution: Joan Robinson (1970), Nicholas Kaldor (1964, 1970, 1980, 1981, 1982, 1983, 1983a), Richard Kahn (1972, 1972a). Although Cambridge economists are well-known, few students of money in North America are aware of their work in the field of money. In a way this is understandable because, until the emergence of Monetarism, Cambridge economists had not really attempted (except for Lord Radcliffe) to distinguish their views on money from the typical textbook interpretation of Hicksian economics.

As a matter of fact, it could be said that American post-Keynesianism has emerged as a reaction to this apparent lack of interest about monetary and financial matters on the part of Cambridge economists. Paul Davidson (1972, 1980) and Hyman Minsky (1976, 1981, 1982) have extensively developed original frameworks for the study of monetary economics which imply a critique of both Monetarist and Cambridge (growth model) economics. More recently, Sidney Weintraub (1978, ch. 4), Basil Moore (1979, 1979a, 1983); and Albert Wojnilower (1977, 1980) have perpetuated this nonorthodox interest in money questions. Although all these authors have been identified with the same national group, some (in particular Wojnilower) are closer to the Cambridge post-Keynesians.

The third group, the economists of the dynamic circuit, which I call the *circuitistes*, has arisen out of discontent with the various reinterpretations of the *General Theory* (Hansen/Lerner, Hicks/Patinkin, Clower/Leijonhufvud) and as a consequence of the abandonment of short-run analysis by neo-Ricardian Cambridge economists. Like the American post-Keynesians, the circuitistes, who are mainly based in France, have developed an interest for monetary studies and policy issues. Of course the idea of an economic circuit is not new. But the circuitistes' attempt to merge the concept of the circuit, as seen by François Perroux (1965) in the work of Joseph Schumpeter (1963), to the insights of Keynes in the *General Theory* and also in the *Treatise on*

Money (1930). The result is a theory of money integrated with a theory of accumulation. Bernard Schmitt (1966, 1972) initiated the quest of the circuitistes. He was followed by Jacqueline Fau (1974), Alain Barrère (1979), Alain Parguez (1975, 1980, 1981, 1981a, 1982, 1983), Bernard Vallageas (1979), Frédéric Poulon (1982), François Rachline (1982), Christian Ottavj (1981, 1982), and Jacques Léonard (1981, 1982), among others.

Also in France appeared a new wave of economists dissatisfied with orthodox monetary economics. Those economists felt that the institutional framework provided by the dominant American-based textbook interpretation of money creation and control could not be applied to the French banking system. Although the point had been made several times before (for instance by Jacques Le Bourva (1959, 1962)), it is only as a result of the sharp distinction provided by John Hicks (another Nobel Laureate, although a reborn one (1975, p. 375)), that a group of French economists, the economists of overdraft economies, has attempted to analyze in a systematic fashion the particularities arising from an economy where firms and commercial banks borrow from commercial banks and the central bank respectively. Hicks (1974, p. 51) called such an economy an *overdraft* sector, whereas economies in which firms or banks could rely on liquid assets were part of an auto-sector. The overdraft view is sometimes called the Banque de France view since many officials or researchers of the French central bank have put it forward: Renaud de La Genière (1981), Pierre Berger (1972, 1975), J.-H. David (1978), G. Maarek (1978). The overdraft approach is now found in advanced French textbooks, for instance in the books of V. Levy-Garboua and B. Weymuller (1979), D. Lacoue-Labarthe (1980) and P.J. Lehman (1979).

Of course the distinctions made above are somewhat arbitrary. They cannot be absolute. Furthermore, there is quite a large number of authors who have presented theses that are perfectly compatible with the main message of the four groups identified above. It would, however, be unreasonable to assimilate them to any one of these groups. Still, their views are also considered in the next section.[5]

2. The Common Viewpoints

The main objective of this section is to show that there exists a large consensus on several key monetary issues; a consensus which extends past the frontiers of differentiated monetary institutions; a consensus which contradicts the "universal" theory propounded by neoclassical or monetarist economists.

For simplification, I shall call *credit-money view* the consensus approach of the post-Keynesians, the circuitistes, and the overdraft economists.

A. Loans Make Deposits

Orthodox monetary economics is founded on the double hypothesis of free reserves and the credit multiplier. Each individual bank may only increase its loans to the public when depositors increase their balances there, i.e., when free cash reserves augment for that one bank. In the aggregate, commercial banks are allowed to make supplementary loans when they dispose of free reserves. The latter can be obtained through modifications of the behavior of the public, as a result of a surplus in the foreign account, as a consequence of the intervention of the central bank on the open market, or following a change in the reserve requirements. Although the credit multiplier functions on the basis of an expansion of credit, *deposits make loans* in the orthodox context. The usual sequence of events is as follows: the central bank buys some security from a member of the public; the deposits of this person are increased; the bank which benefits from these increased deposits now disposes of excess reserves and can make new loans.

All the properties of an excess-money-induced inflation follows naturally from the apparently innocuous postulate that deposits make loans. First, deposits (i.e., money) are the support of purchasing power. They are independent of the credits that could be made by the banks. Whereas households could not use their securities to buy consumer goods, they can utilize their cash deposits without any constaint. There is a creation and a utilization of purchasing power without the equivalent production of goods. Hence the proximate responsibility for inflation lays in the hands of the central bank since it can limit the creation of this purchasing power (money) by supervising the rate of growth of reserves (or high-powered money) through open-market operations (sterilization of foreign currencies, etc.). Whatever happens on the credit side is not considered important. In fact, it cannot be important. If deposits (money) are controlled, purchasing power is controlled, and inflation is under control. Thus say the Monetarists and modern neoclassical Keynesians.

The credit-money view rejects this approach to money and inflation by reversing the sequence of events. According to the unorthodox view, *loans make deposits* (Fau, 1974, p. 26). Banks do not wait for the appropriate amount of liquid resources to exist to provide new loans to the public (mainly firms). Credits are created ex nihilo (Schmitt, 1966, p. 94). The recipient of purchasing power is the initial recipient of the loan. When the bank makes a new loan, the borrower is being immediately credited with a deposit, the amount of which is exactly equal to the amount of the loan. Hence, "the increase in the supply of money is a *consequence* of increased loan expenditure, not the *cause* of it" (Kaldor and Trevithick, 1981, p. 5). The loan is the causal factor.

This explains the name of the *credit-money* view. Money does not arise as a result of the intervention of the central bank. Money is created as a by-product of the loans provided by the Banking System. It is impossible to have one without the other. This fact is particularly clear in the case of the overdraft, which is simply a form of guaranteed loan. When a payment is made through an overdraft, the buyer is subjected to an automatic increase in his debt towards the bank (the used portion of his line of credit is increased) whereas the seller benefits from an equivalent *increase* of his bank deposits. The increase in loans results in an increase in the stock of money.

It is quite easy to understand why French or even British economists would feel particularly at ease with this type of description of the money creation process. In France and Great Britain, but also in other European countries such as Finland (Toullec, 1979, p. 291), the access of firms to liquid resources is not based, as it would be in the textbook auto-economy, on the detention of assets which are easily marketed. Firms are indebted permanently to banks and rely on them for the provision of borrowed financial resources.

But even if the North American financial system is closer to the textbook case, it still cannot be considered solely as being part of an auto-sector. In fact, statistics now show that unused bank credit commitments, i.e., guaranteed unused borrowing and spending capacity, exceed the total quantity of demand deposits in the Unites States (Wojnilower, 1980, p. 289).

It follows that the reserves that North American banks could be required to hold exceed the reserves that they do actually hold. Since the unused bank credit commitments are legally binding, banks have no control upon these potential reserve requirements. Thus even the North American financial system is not part of the auto-economy. It is better described by an analysis founded on the overdraft sector.

B. Deposits Make Reserves

Once commercial banks have created credit money, how do they get hold of the reserves required by the newly created deposits or how do they obtain the currency cash requested by the public? In many European banking systems, France in particular, commercial banks simply borrow their requirements in high-powered money. Most banks are permanently indebted to the central bank.[6] The money market in those circumstances does not play a fundamental role. When banks, overall, are in need of more high-powered money, they increase their borrowings with the central bank at the discount rate set by the latter. Legal reserve ratios, when they exist, are not used to control the created quantity of money. They exist to increase the cost of the loans granted by the banks since reserves carry no interest revenue.[7]

Unless it has set some restrictive credit policy, the central bank is prepared to respond to any increased demand for high-powered money from the Banking System, and this at the interest-rate level which it has chosen as its discount rate (Le Bourva, 1962, p. 39). Thus, as a whole, commercial banks in such a situation do not have to worry about their reserve or currency requirements. They initially decide upon the amount of loans they are ready to grant and worry latter about their liquidity position. In such a system the overall banking system cannot run into liquidity problems, and neither can an individual bank, provided they all increase their assets in step (Le Bourva, 1962, p. 34; Lutz, 1971, p. 147).

It is often claimed that the North American and German banking systems function in quite a different way (Toullec, 1979, p. 294). This however is an illusion. Although institutional arrangements are quite dissimilar, the expansionary process of credit is the same. There are three pieces of evidence. First, as seen in section 2.A, banks grant legally binding lines of credit which imply future access to reserves. Second, North American banks must respond to lagged required reserve-accounting conventions. Third, banks always have access, although limited, to the discount window of the central bank.

It is impossible for North American or German central banks not to provide the required reserves (Moore, 1983, p. 544; Lutz, 1971, p. 146). Credits and their accompanying deposits are on a different time frame. The commercial banks cannot reduce deposits or credits which are subjected to their reserve requirements because the deposits or the credits to which they correspond have been created or guaranteed in the past. Furthermore, whatever the central bank decides *not* to provide on the open market is obtained through the discount window.

Hence, in the North American as in the French financial system, banks first augment their advances and loans and later search for the liquid funds which they are required to hold. Commercial banks must only make sure that they hold a sufficient level of second-rank reserves, which can be traded on the open market or at the discount window (Lutz, 1971, p. 145).[8] It can be said that a third option is open to commercial banks: as a consequence of the lack of reserves they can decide to reduce their outstanding call loans. But this is precisely precluded by the generalization of legally binding credit lines. The Federal Reserve System cannot, any more than the Banque de France, control the emission of high-powered money. It can only modify its discount rate or its rate of intervention on the open market.

Most nonorthodox monetary theorists agree that the central bank cannot directly control the stock of money. The stock of money is caused by, or results from, previously made decisions (those pertaining to credit and loans). To control an aggregate which is a *consequence* rather than a *cause* does not make much sense (Kahn, 1972, pp. 147–48). Even if it were meaningful to control monetary aggregates, to use reserve requirements to do so would not be very efficient. In fact, it is argued that to limit the amount of the money supply is to control the demand for money, i.e., the willingness of the public (mainly households) to hold cash balances. This says nothing of the willingness of banks or of firms to contract loans (Kaldor, 1982, p. 14).

In financial systems of the French type, most attempts to control monetary expansion are based upon extra-market features. Larger collaterals are required from would-be borrowers. Ceilings on bank advances, or on the rate of increase of these advances, have been proposed and used in the past (the *corset* in England). Even controls via interest-rate floors (the closest to a market mechanism) are not thought to be very efficient because it is contended that banks pass over the cost of borrowing to their customers (Levy-Garboua and Levy-Garboua, 1972, p. 281), whereas neither the demand for credit, nor the demand for money, is very sensitive to changes in interest rates, especially in inflationary times, except when those changes are so large that they could disrupt all financial markets.

In North American-type financial systems, it is usually assumed that the central bank intervenes through the open market. But as explained earlier, the efficiency of open-market operations cannot be linked to the control of high-powered money. The reduction of the rate of growth of money must be caused by increased interest rates. But as just argued above, the interest inelasticity of the demand for credit (or money) makes a very poor policy instrument of the rate of interest (Kaldor, 1964, p. 132; Kaldor, 1970, p. 8). Recent American banking history may perhaps demonstrate this point. When Mr. Paul Volcker announced in October 1979 that the Federal Reserve System would pursue quantitative monetary aggregate objectives, the Fed sold spectacular amounts of Treasury bonds on the open market only to find its advances to commercial banks increase by a similar amount. Despite large increases in interest rates, the Fed judged that its conventional market actions were not sufficient to fulfill its targets. In March 1980, it introduced credit controls under the form of loan-growth ceilings. These were "startlingly potent" (Wojnilower, 1980, p. 307). This shows that a radically efficient control of the money supply cannot rely on market mechanisms, whether in the overdraft sector or in the auto-sector.

To sum up, it can be said that in normal times commercial banks are ready to provide all loans, and central banks are ready to provide all reserves or advances, which are demanded at the existing interest rate. This is true in North American as well as in French types of banking systems. Loans make deposits and deposits make reserves. The money supply is endogenous at the rate of interest fixed by the central bank or the Banking System. It can be represented by an horizontal supply-curve at the given rate of interest.

One of the most important consequences is that the growth of the money stock cannot be held as the culprit of modern inflation (Moore, 1979, pp. 32–33). The stock of money is neither a proximate cause of inflation nor a remote one. Inflation must be linked to speculative or nonproductive *credit* (Loranger, 1983; Léonard, 1982, p. 547), or else to excessive wage-settlements (Kahn, 1972, p. 138; Weintraub, 1978, ch. 9).

These are the main points upon which agreement can be *generally* reached. When one goes into more detailed arguments or when further implications are drawn, there is no universal theory any more.

3. Points of Differentiation

We will now attempt to explain a series of items which raise some doubts among credit-money economists. Answering these questions allows me to show a few more important characteristics of credit-money.

A. Overdraft Economists Versus Others

There are mainly two points of disagreement between the overdraft economists and the other representatives of nonorthodox monetary theory presented here. The first disagreement concerns the domain of validity of the overdraft sector. Overdraft economists express their dissatisfaction with the monetary theory presented in textbooks because they think it does not apply to their particular institutional framework, not because they reject the theory. As Hicks (1974, p. 51) once thought, overdraft economists believe that there are countries, such as the United States or Germany, where orthodox theory can be applied. Post-Keynesians and circuitistes, on the other hand, reject textbook monetary economics on the grounds that it depicts a mythical economy which does not exist anywhere.[9] For post-Keynesians and circuitistes, the relations established by the overdraft economists are valid in overdraft economies *and* in the so-called auto or market economies. Institutions may be different in France and in Great Britain or in the United States, but the financial systems of all these countries exhibit the same basic properties, the same links between loans, deposits, reserves, and interest rates.

The second point of disagreement follows from the first one. Since overdraft economists believe that there are some economies functioning according to the rules of the market, *some* of these economists infer that there must exist some optimal financial system where the creation of money is the result of a proper equilibrating market mechanism. In these "natural" economies, which would resemble the North American financial system, the financial market allocates the available saving funds of the households to the most productive projects of the firms. The flexibility of market interest-rates insures the coherence between advances to firms and planned savings of households (Lacoue-Labarthe, 1980, p. 425).

As pointed out by Parguez (1981, pp. 418–19), such a theory is built on Hayekian premises. It is assumed that it is possible to have an economy without credit money. Due to existing credit arrangements and the intervention of the central bank, and in the absence of the proper market mechanisms, interest rates may become too low in an overdraft economy (Thomas, 1981, p. 147). As a consequence, investment expenditures cannot all be financed by households' savings. Some firms must finance capital through the creation of ex nihilo credit. This capital cannot be sufficiently productive. Maarek (1978) explains this best. He quotes Hayek, uses a Hayekian circuit, and compares realized monetary interest-rates to a natural interest-rate. Credit money is thus considered to be an anomaly which generates disequilibrium and inflation. In a true market economy, with no credit money, household savings determine investment. The decisions of firms are constrained by previously accumulated households' savings (Levy-Garboua and Weymuller, 1979, p. 176).[10] All decisions are then optimal.

This contrasts with the views of the post-Keynesians and those of the circuitistes. Both groups emphasize the causality from investment to savings as presented by Keynes. Previous savings can never constrain the possible amount of investment (Parguez, 1981; Davidson, 1980; Ranson, 1983). Increased production requires increased finance. The latter can only be forthcoming if the Banking System allows more loans. Credit money is a requirement of the economic system. It is not a parasite of the system.

B. Finance: Money or Loans?

Although all post-Keynesian and circuitistes agree that "the investment market can become congested through shortage of cash" and that "it can never become congested through shortage of saving" (Keynes, 1973, p. 222), there is much confusion as to what *cash* really means. For Keynes, *cash* or *finance* means a stock of money required by planned or realized economic activity. A planned increase in output, whether in capital goods or in consumption goods, generally requires an increase in finance (Keynes, 1973, pp. 220 and 229). Keynes is quite clear that finance is money, not credit, or at least that the two are not necessarily the same (Keynes, 1973, p. 207). Of all economists, Davidson (1972, ch. 7) is probably the closest to Keynes. For Davidson, finance is money, and it may be obtained either through loans from the Banking System (an expansion of the money supply) or through the reduction of households' money balances via higher interest rates (with a constant stock of money). Davidson devotes a whole chapter of his book to the finance motive.

Other post-Keynesians and circuitistes do not attach such a large importance to the finance of planned expenditures. This must be attributed to the fact that they mainly pay attention to an economy organized under the overdraft system. As a consequence, firms get their liquid resources secured through the extension of lines of credit. Planned activity is taken care of by the availability of unused credit facilities. When the idle part of the credit line is finally triggered, i.e., when new expenditures are met, "there will be an automatic increase in the money supply for the simple reason that additional expenditure will swell the bank deposits of the recipient" (Kaldor and Trevithick, 1981, p. 6). This explains the frequent assimilation of credit with money as has been noticed by Loranger (1983, p. 28, fn. 3).

It follows that most post-Keynesian or circuitistes see finance as a flow of credit. They recognize that expenditures must eventually be financed by the transfer of funds into demand deposits. But the stock of these funds at any point in time is considered to be a residual. It cannot have any direct significance. Loans and advances from banks, on the other hand, have a direct significance. The circuitistes, in particular, view finance as a flow of money-debt, issued by the banks to producers, for the latter to remunerate their workers or to buy their new assets (Parguez 1975, p. 106). This flow of money-debt is being extinguished when the producers pay back their loans as a result of consumers' expenditures and the collection of their savings. The part of the flow which cannot be extinguished increases the existing stock of money (Bouvier and Gaubert, 1976, p. 63). It corresponds to the savings which households (or firms) want to keep under the form of money balances (de Mourgues, 1978, p. 77).[11]

This may help us to understand the importance which circuitistes attach to the distinction between the flow of endogenous money and the conventional stock of (residual) money (Parguez, 1983, p. 9; Parguez, 1975, p. 111; Lavoie, 1984, 1984a). All business expenditures must be financed by a renewed flow of credit money (Rachline, 1982). What is essential for the proper functioning of the economy is the credit money which businesses are required to have access to when they distribute income. The importance of money cannot be assessed by the part of the flow which is being hoarded (Chick, 1981, p. 195).

Although Cambridge post-Keynesians present their arguments in a different manner, they also view the importance of money from its credit side, as a flow of bank loans. The same can clearly be said of Wojnilower (1980) in the United States.[12] Most of their views are incorporated in the Radcliffe report, which is not, contrary to Samuelson's judgment, the most sterile operation of all times. As noted by A.B. Cramp (1971, p. 64), orthodox monetary theory "focuses attention on the *stock* of money while Radcliffism emphasises the *flow* of credit." This opposition is sometimes linked to the famous controversy between the Currency Principle and the Banking Principle (Cramp, 1962; Levy-Garboua and Weymuller, 1979, p. 192).

Most of the evidence put forward by the Radcliffe committee, however, was rather vague, as it attempted to discard the quantitative equation by the argument of unstable velocity of circulation. There were several references to the effect that the stock of money was not a "reliable policy measure," or that what was of relevance was "the whole liquidity position."[13] But in his memorandum to the committee, Kahn was quite explicit: "There always must be a monetary policy. . . . It is best expressed in terms of rates of interest on loans of various maturities and of the amount of bank advances" (1972, p. 128). And later he added: "The Committee should view with suspicion any line of argument which attributes to the behavior of the supply of money a significance of its own, apart from its relationship with rates of interest and bank advances" (1972, p. 147–48).

This point of view is endorsed by American post-Keynesians, for instance Eichner, who says that "it is credit throughout the economy—that becomes the critical monetary factor in a post-Keynesian short-period model, not the stock of money" (1979, p. 40). The preceding is summarized quite sarcastically by Wojnilower: "I can testify that to all . . . the money stock—in contrast to oil or credit—is a meaningless abstraction" (1980, p. 324).

The emphasis on the flow of credit, and on the decisions of those who increase their liabilities, should underline the artificial static character of traditional portfolio theory. In the latter, adjustments of assets by their holders in reaction to changes in the stocks of monetary assets (however defined) are explained. But the most realistic analysis of change cannot be done at a point in time, with a given stock of wealth (Cramp, 1971, pp. 64–66). Changes in the money supply are generally induced by dynamic forces which are associated with the flow of loans which are available to producers. Finance is credit. In that sense, most post-Keynesian and circuitistes are drifting away from Keynes' previous claims.[14]

C. *Is Money Really an Endogenous Variable?*

It should now be obvious that the monetary framework described by Keynes in the *General Theory*, or immediately after, is incompatible with the financial system analyzed by credit-money economists. For one, Keynes' emphasis on an exogenous stock of money precludes such merging. This point is now generally recognized by all parties (Kaldor, 1982, p. 21; Hicks, 1982, p. 264). Joan Robinson gives an excellent explanation of Keynes' propensity to take a next-to-orthodox stance:

> "It would have been much simpler to start by assuming a constant rate of interest and a perfectly elastic supply of money. But then his whole case would have been dismissed as a misunderstanding of the orthodox position. He was obliged to accept the presumptions of his critics in order to explode them from within" (1970, p. 507).

It follows that those economists who desire to perpetuate Keynesian tradition may not manage to completely evade the traps of orthodox theory. There are several instances among post-Keynesians. The two main points of issue are as follows: 1.) money is not endogenous; and 2.) interest rates must rise when the level of activity rises. The confusion created by the colliding programs of research is so great that some authors adopt opposite views at different times. For example, Edward Nell proposes a defense of Keynes based on the hypothesis of an endogenous money supply (1979, p. 210), only to later present a Keynesian model of investment where the supply of money is fixed and interest rates rise with investment (1983, p. 100). Victoria Chick sometimes claims that the central bank can control the stock of money by pursuing offensive rather than defensive policies (1977, p. 89), while on the other hand she acknowledges that "about the most the [Central] Bank can do is manipulate the interest rate" (1983, p. 236). Sidney Weintraub concludes that there can be "a good deal of both 'endogeneity' and 'exogeneity' in [the Monetary Authorities'] actions" (1978, p. 75).

Sheila Dow and Peter Earl (1982), in their book on the Keynesian monetary approach, do not even mention the endogenous-money hypothesis.

The most baffling is probably Paul Davidson. On one hand, he recognizes that the money supply can be increased endogenously. He calls this the income-generating/finance process (1972, p. 226). But on the other hand, he asserts that monetary authorities can control the stock of money (1972, p. 227). Since Davidson is the author who has provided the most detailed analysis of the creation of money, his work is open to criticism.

Davidson (like the circuitistes) shows that even when firms manage to sell everything they produce, they are bound to face a financial-flow deficit, owing to the fact that households keep part of their savings under the form of money balances. Davidson calls this the case of negative excess flow-demand for securities. The financial-flow deficit of firms is larger than the amount which households are ready to take on directly by buying securities (shares or bonds) (1972, p. 325). Davidson, however, leaves the reader under the impression that the Banking System has the power to restrict the appearance of these money balances (1972, p. 327). There is some incoherence here. Davidson admits that "at the beginning of the period," firms are in need of finance which is provided for by an increase in the money supply because of bank borrowing (1972, pp. 322–23). At the end of the period, when households come to decide on which portion of their income they wish to keep as money deposits, the money supply is already enlarged. Credit money is already created to allow firms to distribute incomes. The decisions of the households with regard to these incomes can only reduce the newly created stock of money. So how can the Banking System restrain deposits at this stage? Furthermore, Davidson does not show how the monetary authorities would stop the banks from increasing the money supply in general, unless there are direct restrictions on loans.

It seems that these instances of confusion result from too great a desire to stick to Keynes' portfolio approach and to his vertically given money-supply. As Hicks shows, in modern credit-money economies the open-market policy of the central bank is impotent from a quantitative point of view. But it can still control interest rates: "If the Bank tries to avoid coming to the rescue, interest rates will shoot up; still at some point, it will have to come to the rescue" (1982, p. 264).

D. The Determination of the Interest Rate

Keynes' liquidity-preference theory is well known. Post-Keynesians do not abide by it anymore, however.[15] Before discussing the different ideas which have been advanced to explain the level of interest rates within a credit-money economy, I would like to deal with those analyses which seem to suggest that the level of interest rates increases with activity, in particular Hyman Minsky's hypothesis of systemic fragility (1976, ch. 5–6; 1982). According to Minsky, capitalism is inherently flawed; our financial systems lead to periods of inflation or depressions. A main reason, it appears, is that "the financing needs of the investment boom raise interest rates" (1982, p. 124).[16] According to Minsky, this seems to be the result of both the rapid increase in the demand for financing (1982, p. 140) and the abandonment of safe assets consequent to euphoric expectations (1982, p. 123).

This explanation borders on the lack-of-savings thesis and is quite contrary to both post-Keynesian monetary theory and Keynes' view of the trade cycle. In chapter 23 of the *General Theory*, Keynes makes it quite clear that rises in interest rates were consequential to the crisis. They were not the cause of it. From the post-Keynesian point of view, there are no natural forces that should provoke increases in interest rates, since interest rates are not the result of ordinary supply and demand forces. The Banking System cannot restrain the amount of cash balances which households desire to hold. Interest rates do not usually rise as a consequence of natural forces. They rise because the monetary authorities want them to do so. The most that could be admitted is that banks and the central bank are constantly pressured in a boom period to provide further liquidity at a given price. Interest rates could rise as a result of omission (Cramp, 1971, p. 66).

The argument usually put forward in favor of this modified excess demand for loanable funds theory is that the new loans, which are conducive to credit money, may lead to an excess of money supply (Chaineau, 1977, p. 15; Minsky, 1982, p. 140; Coghlan 1978, p. 17; Chick 1983, p. 237). This excess supply of money, through the usual monetarist mechanisms, generates an excessive aggregate demand with the ensuing inflation. To fight it off, the monetary authorities would decide to raise interest rates and restrain credit. The only trouble with such an explanation is that within an overdraft economy there can never be an excess supply of money. The recipients of such an excess would use it to diminish their liabilities and the money so used would be "extinguished as a result of the repayment of bank debt" (Kaldor and Trevithick, 1981, p. 7). In fact, this is what happens in practice (Berger, 1975, p. 156). It also explains why post-Keynesians argue that government deficits and a favorable balance of payments have no (direct) effect on the creation of money (Kaldor, 1983a, p. 87; Le Bourva, 1962, pp. 48–50). The creation of high-powered money which eventually results from these two situations is compensated by the reduction in the needs of commercial banks for high-powered money. This is the so-called compensation thesis (Berger, 1972; Arnoul, 1977, pp. 136–47).

So if market forces are excluded, what determines the rate of interest? Credit-money economists do not give very precise answers. For instance, Kahn (1972a, p. 94) points to "a lack of uniqueness in the correlation between the quantity of bank credit and its price." There are in fact two broad answers. The first one links the rate of interest to the requirements of the external balance (Kaldor, 1982, p. 24; de La Genière, 1981, p. 275). The central bank adjusts its discount rate or its rate of intervention on the open market to the rates of interest abroad or to the rate of exchange of its foreign currency reserves, or to any such external variable.

The second answer sees the rate of interest as the result of a coalition between the bankers (including the central bank) who set the rates on loans and the rentiers whose savings are being continuously revalued on the stock market. Thus, the rate of interest is not the market result of a confrontation of the liquidity preference of the banks versus the liquidity preference of the public (Keynes, 1973, p. 219), nor the variable which equates the supply and the demand of money (as orthodox economics would have it), since there is no market as such (Lacoue-Labarthe, 1980, p. 413). The rate of interest is the result of a convention (Townsend, 1937), a consensus between those who can manipulate and those who can benefit from interest rates.[17] It is a measure of the confidence of the financial system, a measure of the time horizon of its speculative activity (Parguez, 1981, p. 442). The central bank, within some margin, is free to ratify or to modify the rate set by the financial cartel coalition.[18]

3. Conclusion

Credit-money theory leaves no room for the monitoring of conventional monetary aggregates. What ought to be controlled and for what purpose? A monetary policy should aim for sustained rates of growth, with steady or moderately rising prices, and without sudden collapses of the financial system. The main goal suggests that bank credit should be freely available, at low interest rates (Keynes, 1930, vol. 2, p. 217). The threat of inflation implies that the control of credit aggregates or of the quality of credit may be required to restrain runaway inflation owing to speculative activity. But since this may lead to endogenous financial crises, some alternative regulation may be thought of, some refurbished version of Regulation Q, where interest-rate ceilings are being imposed upon banks and financial intermediaries (Wojnilower, 1977, p. 237; Wojnilower, 1980, p. 324). As defined above, monetary policy matters.

Notes

1. There is some irony here, since Sraffa's later works did not deal with money in any way.

2. I am of course referring to Gérard Debreu and Kenneth Arrow. The theory of rational expectations belongs to a similar kind of methodology. Another example is Frank Hahn (1982) who, in an otherwise excellent book, manages to write 100 pages on money and inflation without ever mentioning the role of banks.

3. See Victoria Chick (1981, p. 177). This is also Leijonhufvud's position: "Most astoundingly, Neoclassical Keynesianism has ended up in a position that has proven difficult to demarcate from Monetarism in any signficiant way" (1981, p. 179).

4. Samuelson is not alone here. Leijonhufvud may again be quoted: "... Cambridge Keynesians since the death of Keynes have shown no further interest to speak of in monetary theory. ... [It] is seen as a dead-end street" (1981, p. 176).

5. One can think of Alan Holmes (1969), Raymond Lombra and Raymond Torto (1973), Edgar Feige and Robert McGee (1977), and Baldwin Ranson (1983) in the United States; Richard Coghlan (1978, 1981) and Victoria Chick (1977, 1981, 1983) in Great Britain; Jacques Le Bourva (1959, 1962), Jean Denizet (1970), and Jean-Gabriel Thomas (1981) in France; Friedrich Lutz (1971), Gunnar Heinsohn and Otto Steiger (1982) in Germany.

6. In France, some banks are specialized in providing loans while others specialize in collecting deposits (Toullec, 1979, p. 198). The money market exists to balance the two (David, 1978, p. 2191). In the text, I refer to the former banks.

7. Although the preceding footnote shows that legal reserves on loans could not be very efficient, in France there have been reserve requirements on increases in loans. See the discussion by Paul-Jacques Lehman (1979, pp. 79–93).

8. In my opinion, this is the significance of the impact of the ratio of bank loans to bank deposits on the liquidity of the financial system (Eichner, 1979, p. 46).

9. Heinsohn and Steiger (1982) demonstrate magnificently that modern credit economies did not evolve from commodity-money economies.

10. This view is clearly linked to the shortage of savings (SOS) hypothesis, which is criticized by Davidson (1980, p. 287–).

11. Exactly the same approach is adopted by the governor of the Banque de France, Renaud de La Genière (1981, p. 271).

12. Moore (1979, 1983), like all credit-money economists, points out that the stock of money is the consequence of previous loans. In his presentation, however, bank advances seem to be of a temporary nature and for working-capital (wages mainly) purposes only (1983, p. 546).

13. This is Kaldor's criticism of the Radcliffe report (1982, pp. 8–9). It must be added that Kaldor himself, in his memorandum to the committee in 1958, initially argued against Monetarism on the basis of a variable velocity of circulation (1964). Only in 1970 did he clearly embrace a credit-money approach.

14. The reader must be made aware, however, that at the end of his second article on the finance motive, Keynes admits that planned activity may have no effect on the demand for money or interest rates as a consequence of the overdraft, recognizing implicitly that the demand for money for business purposes is directly obtained via credit arrangements (Keynes, 1973, pp. 219, 223).

15. Neither did Keynes in his own time! This point is brought forward by Kaldor (1981, pp. 12–13).

16. The Minsky hypothesis is analyzed in more detail in Lavoie (1983, pp. 297–313). Kalecki (1969, pp. 14–15) advances the same idea, claiming that interest rates must rise for (unspecified) technical monetary reasons, although he emphasizes that a sufficient amount of savings will always be forthcoming.

17. For Hicks (1982, pp. 270–72), the deposit rate of the bank is the base of the interest-rate structure. Such a rate is clearly under the control of the bankers and the rentiers.

18. This second answer has mainly arisen from verbal discussions with professors Alain Parguez and Mario Seccareccia.

References

Arnoul, E. 1977. *Espace national et déséquilibre monétaire*. Paris, Presses Universitaires de France.

Barrère, A. 1979. *Déséquilibres économiques et contre-révolution keynésienne*. Paris, Economica.

Berger, P. 1972. Rapports entre l'évolution de la balance des paiements et l'évolution de la liquidité interne. In: André de Lattre and P. Berger, (eds.), *Monnaie et balance des paiements*. Paris, Armand Colin.

Berger, P. 1975. Émission monétaire et multiplicateur de crédit. In: *Essais en l'honneur de Jean Marchal*, volume 2. Paris, Cujas.

Bharadwaj, K. 1983. On Effective Demand: Certain Recent Critiques. In: J.A. Kregel, (ed.), *Distribution, Effective Demand and International Economic Relations*. London, Macmillan.

Bouvier, G.-Y. and P. Gaubert. 1976. *Offre de monnaie. Politique monétaire*. Paris, Presses Universitaires de France.

Chaineau, A. 1977. *La mécanique de l'équilibre économique*. Paris, Presses Universitaires de France.

Chick, V. 1977. *The Theory of Monetary Policy*. Oxford, Parkgate Books.

Chick, V. 1981. On the Structure of the Theory of Monetary Policy. In: D. Currie, R. Nobay, and D. Peel, (eds.), *Macroeconomic Analysis: Essays in Macroeconomics and Econometrics*. London, Croom Helm.

Chick, V. 1983. *Macroeconomics After Keynes: A Reconsideration of the General Theory*. Oxford, Philip Allan.

Coghlan, R. 1978. A New View of Money. *Lloyds Bank Review*, July.

Coghlan, R. 1981. *Money, Credit and the Economy*. London, Allen and Unwin.

Cramp, A. B. 1962. Two Views on Money. *Lloyds Bank Review*, July.

Cramp, A. B. 1971. Monetary Policy: Strong or Weak? In: N. Kaldor, (ed.), *Conflicts in Policy Objectives*. Oxford, Basil Blackwell. Reprinted from *Lloyds Bank Review* (October, 1970).

David, J.-H. 1978. "Structures bancaires et contrôle monétaire: le cas de la France." *Economies et Sociétés*, 12, (10-12).

Davidson, P. 1972. *Money and the Real World*. London, Macmillan.

Davidson, P. 1980. Is There a Shortage of Savings in the United States? The Role of Financial Institutions, Monetary and Fiscal Policy in Capital Accumulation

During Periods of Stagflation. In: *Special Study on Economic Change*, vol. 4, for the Joint Economic Committee of the Congress of the United States. Washington, DC, U.S. Government Printing Office.

Denizet, J. 1969. *Monnaie et financement*. Paris, Dunod.

Dow, S. C and P. E. Earl. 1982. *Money Matters: A Keynesian Approach to Monetary Economics*. Oxford, Martin Robertson.

Eichner, A. S. 1979. A Post-Keynesian Short-Period Model. *Journal of Post-Keynesian Economics*, Summer.

Fau, J. 1974. *Le circuit économique social*. Paris, Cujas.

Feige, E. and R. McGee. 1977. Money Supply Control and Lagged Reserve Accounting. *Journal of Money, Credit and Banking*, November.

Friedman, M. 1969. The Optimum Quantity of Money. In: *The Optimum Quantity of Money and Other Essays*, Chicago, Aldine.

Hahn, F. H. 1982. *Money and Inflation*. Oxford, Basil Blackwell.

Hayek, F. 1967. *Prices and Production*. New York, Augustus M. Kelley. [1931].

Heinsohn, G. and O. Steiger. 1982. Private Property Debts and Interest Or: The Origin of Money and the Rise and Fall of Monetary Economies. University of Bremen, 55 pp. Working paper to be published in *Studi Economici*.

Henry, J. 1982. Les méthodes post-keynésiennes et l'approche post-classique. *Actualité économique*, January.

Hicks, J. 1974. *The Crisis in Keynesian Economics*. Oxford, Basil Blackwell.

Hicks, J. 1975. Revival of Political Economy: The Old and the New. *Economic Record*, September.

Hicks, J. 1982. *Money, Interest and Wages*. Cambridge, Harvard University Press.

Holmes, A. 1969. Operational Constraints on the Stabilization of Money Supply Growth. In: *Controlling Monetary Aggregates*. Boston, Federal Reserve Bank of Boston.

Kahn, R. F. 1972. Memorandum of Evidence Submitted to the Radcliffe Committee (1958). In: *Selected Essays on Employment and Growth*. Cambridge, Cambridge University Press.

Kahn, R. F. 1972a. Some Notes on Liquidity Preference. In: *Selected Essays on Employment and Growth*. Cambridge, Cambridge University Press.

Kaldor, N. 1964. Monetary Policy, Economic Stability and Growth. In: *Essays on Economic Policy*. London, Duckworth.

Kaldor, N. 1970. The New Monetarism. *Lloyds Bank Review*, July.

Kaldor, N. 1980. Monetarism and U.K. Monetary Policy. *Cambridge Journal of Economics*, December.

Kaldor, N. 1981. *Origins of the New Monetarism*. Cardiff, University College Press.

Kaldor, N. 1982. *The Scourge of Monetarism*. Oxford, Oxford University Press.

Kaldor, N. 1983. *Limitations of the 'General Theory*. London, The British Academy.

Kaldor, N. 1983a. *The Economic Consequences of Mrs. Thatcher*. London, Duckworth.

Kaldor, N. and J. Trevithick. 1981. A Keynesian Perspective on Money. *Lloyds Bank Review*, January.
Kalecki, Michal. 1969. *Studies in the Theory of Business Cycles: 1933–1939*. Oxford, Basil Blackwell.
Keynes, J. M. 1930. *A Treatise on Money*. London, Macmillan.
Keynes, J. M. 1936. *The General Theory of Employment, Interest and Money*. London, Macmillan.
Keynes, J. M. 1973. *The Collected Writings of John Maynard Keynes*. Volume 14. London, Macmillan.
Kurz, H. 1983. What is Wrong with Keynesian Economics? In: J.A. Kregel, (ed.), *Distribution, Effective Demand and International Economic Relations*. London, Macmillan.
Lacoue-Labarthe, Dominique. 1980. *Analyse monétaire*. Paris, Dunod.
de La Genière, Renaud. 1981. Les fondements de la politique monétaire. *Banque*, March.
Lavoie, Marc. 1983. Loi de Minsky et loi d'entropie. *Économie appliquée*, 36 (no. 2–3).
Lavoie, M. 1984. The Endogenous Flow of Credit and the Post-Keynesian Theory of Money. *Journal of Economic Issues*, September.
Lavoie, M. 1984a. Un modèle d'économie monétaire fondé sur la théorie du circuit. *Économie et Sociétés* (to be published).
Le Bourva, Jacques. 1959. La théorie de l'inflation, le rapport des experts et l'opération de décembre 1958. *Revue économique*, September.
Le Bourva, J. 1962. Création de la monnaie et multiplicateur du crédit. In: *Revue économique*, January.
Lehman, P.-J. 1979. *Le système des réserves obligatoires et le contrôle de la masse monétaire*. Paris, Presses Universitaires de France.
Leijonhufvud, A. 1981. *Information and Coordination: Essays in Macroeconomic Theory*. New York, Oxford University Press.
Léonard, J. 1981. Remarques sur le statut de la théorie des prix dans la 'Théorie Générale' de Keynes. *Revue d'économie politique*, November.
Léonard, J. 1982. Politique monétaire et économie monétaire: unité ou conflit? *Économie appliquée*, 35 (no. 3)
Levy-Garboua, L. and V. Levy-Garboua. 1972. Le comportement bancaire, le diviseur de crédit et l'efficacité du contrôle monétaire. *Revue économique*, March.
Levy-Garboua, V. and B. Weymuller. 1979. *Macroéconomie contemporaine*. Paris, Economica.
Lombra, R. E. and R. G. Torto. 1973. Federal Reserve 'Defensive' Behavior and the Reserve Causation Argument. *Southern Economic Journal*, July.
Loranger, J.-G. 1983. La théorie qualitative de la monnaie: quelques résultats économétriques pour l'ensemble de l'économie canadienne. Working paper 8332. Montreal, University of Montreal, Department of Economics, 33 pp.
Lucas, R. E. 1981. Tobin and Monetarism: A Review Article. *Journal of Economic Literature*, June.

Lutz, F. 1971. La création de monnaie par les banques. *Banque*, February.

Maarek, G. 1978. Monnaie et inflation dans une économie d'endettement. *Revue d'économie politique*, January.

Minsky, H. P. 1976. *John Maynard Keynes*. London, Macmillan.

Minsky, H. P. 1981. James Tobin's Asset Accumulation and Economic Activity: A Review Article. In: *Eastern Economic Journal*, July–October.

Minsky, H. P. 1982. *Can 'It' Happen Again? Essays on Instability and Finance*. Armonk, NY, M. E. Sharpe.

Moore, B. 1979. Monetary Factors. In: A.S. Eichner. (ed.), *A Guide to Post-Keynesian Economics*. White Plains, NY, M. E. Sharpe.

Moore, B. 1979a. The Endogenous Money Stock. *Journal of Post-Keynesian Economics*, Fall.

Moore, B. 1983. Unpacking the Post-Keynesian Black Box: Bank Lending and the Money Supply. *Journal of Post-Keynesian Economics*, Summer.

de Mourgues, M. 1978. Structures financières et inflation. *Revue d'économie politique*, January.

Nell, E. J. 1979. Keynes as New Dawn. *Social Research*, Summer.

Nell, E. J. 1983. Keynes after Sraffa: The Essential Properties of Keynes's Theory of Interest and Money. In: J.A. Kregel, (ed.), *Distribution, Effective Demand and International Economic Relations*. London, Macmillan.

Ottavj, C. 1981. Circuit économique et déséquilibre. *Cahiers d'économie politique*, 6.

Ottavj, C. 1982. La monnaie de crédit: une monnaie dirigée. *Économie appliquée*, 35 (no. 3).

Parguez, A. 1975. *Monnaie et macroéconomie*. Paris, Economica.

Parguez, A. 1980. Profit, épargne investissement: éléments pour une théorie monétaire du profit. *Économie appliquée*, 33 (no. 2).

Parguez, A. 1981. Ordre social, monnaie et régulation. *Économie appliquée*, 34 (no. 2–3).

Parguez, A. 1981a. Keynes et la révolution. *Cahiers d'économie politique*, 6, 171–87.

Parguez, A. 1982. La monnaie dans le circuit ou le voile déchiré. *Économie appliquée*, 35 (no. 3).

Parguez, A. 1983. Money and Financial Money Capital within a Keynesian Framework. Paper presented at the colloquium: "Keynes aujourd'hui: théories et politiques." Paris, September, 1983.

Perroux, F. 1965. La théorie pure de la dynamique capitaliste. In: *La pensée économique de Joseph Schumpeter*. Geneva, Droz.

Poulon, F. 1982. Théorie des économies d'endettement et théorie du circuit. *Économie appliquée*, 35 (no. 3).

Rachline, F. 1982. La nature de la monnaie. *Revue économique*, May.

Ranson, B. 1983. The Unrecognized Revolution in the Theory of Capital Formation. *Journal of Economic Issues*, December.

Robinson, J. V. 1970. Quantity Theories Old and New, A Comment. *Journal of Money, Credit and Banking*, November.

Samuelson, P. 1969. The Role of Money in National Economic Policy. In: *Controlling Monetary Aggregates*. Boston, Federal Reserve Bank of Boston.

Schmitt, B. 1966. La monnaie au centre de la répartition. *Revue d'économie politique*, January.

Schmitt, B. 1972. *Macroeconomic Theory*. Albeuve, Switzerland, Castella.

Schumpeter, J. 1963. *Theory of Economic Development*. New York, Oxford University Press. [1934].

Sraffa, P. 1932. Dr. Hayek on Money and Capital. *Economic Journal*, March.

Thomas, J.-G. 1981. Illusion monétaire et illusions monétaristes. *Revue d'économie politique*, 91 (no. 6).

Toullec, C. 1979. Economie de marché, économie d'endettement et politique monétaire. *Banque*, March.

Townsend, H. 1937. Liquidity-premium and the Theory of Value. *Economic Journal*, March.

Vallageas, B. 1979. Réflexions sur les fondements de l'analyse en termes de circuit. *Revue d'économie politique*, 91 (no. 2).

Weintraub, S. 1978. *Capitalism's Inflation and Unemployment Crisis*. Reading, MA, Addison Wesley.

Wojnilower, A. M. 1977. L'envoi. In: E.I. Altman and A.W. Sametz, (eds.), *Financial Crises: Institutions in a Fragile Environment*. New York, John Wiley and Sons.

Wojnilower, A. M. 1980. *The Central Role of Credit Crunches in Recent Financial History. Brookings Papers on Economic Activity*, no. 2.

5 INSTABILITY, CRISIS, AND THE LIMITS OF POLICY MAKING

Jane Knodell and David Levine

1. Introduction

Beginning with the classical school, the predominant view among economists has been that the virtue of a private enterprise economy depends upon its ability to regulate itself and operate as a self-sustaining organization. The importance of self-regulation stems, of course, from a link between private interest and public good. Modern economists (of the neoclassical school) tend to equate the public good with the satisfaction of private interests, making self-regulation desirable precisely because it eliminates any goals for the economy not defined by private persons acting in pursuit of their particular ends. The classical economics of Adam Smith still distinguished between private ends and public good, but considered the pursuit of private ends to be the only effective way of accomplishing the public good.

This view of the economy defines the role of government as that of providing the necessary institutional context for sustaining the free market. For both the classical and neoclassical economists, this institutional context was distinctly bare. The state has the obligation of protecting the institution of private property from both internal and external threats. Beyond the defense of private property, the state could pursue those projects which were necessary to economic intercourse, but beyond the capacities of private agents (e.g., dams and highways).

Evidently, the idea of the self-regulating market does not leave room for policy in the usual sense of the term. In order to make the idea of policy meaningful, we need to think of the government pursuing specifically economic goals, within the context of a free market economy, which that economy, taken by itself, will not accomplish. But, this way of thinking only makes sense when the goals of government are consistent with the inherent nature of a free market economy. The idea of policy is doubly constrained: on one side by the necessity of defining goals for the economy which the economy does not automatically accomplish and, on the other side, by the necessity of defining goals consistent with what a free market economy has the capacity to accomplish.

Keynes resolves this dilemma by arguing that a free market economy, left to its own devices, will fail to accomplish precisely those ends which it has organized itself to accomplish. In particular, Keynes argues that a free market, rather than facilitating, will impede the pursuit of private ends (and associated public good). In other words, a system with no raison d'être other than setting loose its members to pursue their self-interest, and made up of nothing more than those individuals acting in pursuit of their self-interest, becomes the primary obstacle to the satisfaction of those interests. The self-ordering market becomes the self-disordering market.

This result leaves room for the idea of policy because it allows for the government to pursue specifically economic goals which are well defined even within the context of free markets and private enterprise. The debate over policy pits the Keynesian view on one side, which defines the problem in terms which make the idea of policy meaningful, against the more traditional views within which the idea of policy has little meaning. Thus, the development of economic theory divides into two conceptions of the relation of government to economy: 1.) the classical view, which defines the problem as one of determining the necessary institutional framework; and 2.) the Keynesian view, which defines the problem as one of policy.

The modern idea of government as a policy-making institution requires a breakdown in the ability of the free market to accomplish its ends on its own terms. But, the idea of policy making goes a step further than this. It also carries with it the implication that adjustments in the operation of the market, brought about by the government, are also brought about at the discretion of the government. In other words, these adjustments are not automatic and are not built into the institutional structure of government. To this extent, they depend upon policy decisions which cannot but involve political considerations. Thus, the modern idea that the relation of government to economy involves policy making differs from the classical idea on two grounds: 1.) they differ over their conclusions regarding the ability of the market to regulate itself; and 2.) they differ over the part which discretion should play in the pursuit of economic objectives on the part of the state.

Keynes makes the largest contribution to the breakdown of the idea of self-regulation. His critique focuses upon two fundamental aspects of the operation of a private enterprise economy: 1.) the role of speculation; and 2.) the link between income and employment. Speculation, which is implied in the organization of financial markets within a capitalist economy, sets in motion cumulative processes which tend to disorganize the monetary system and threaten the circulation of commodities. The link between income and employment creates the multiplier process which sustains cumulative movements within what Keynes calls the industrial circulation. Keynes focuses upon the problem of instability and economic fluctuations as forms of disorganization which so threaten the capacity of the market to accomplish its own ends that they justify the intervention of the government in pursuit of precisely those ends.

What, for Keynes, makes stability so essential to the life of a market economy? The answer has to do with the implications of instability for expectations and the role of expectations in investment.

The growth of a private enterprise economy takes place in two dimensions—the trend and the cycle. If firms determine their investment plans upon the basis of long-period considerations, those plans will, taken as a whole, establish the basis for the rate at which the economy expands through time. If firms execute investment plans in a smooth and homogeneous pattern across time, aggregate growth will also be smooth and homogeneous. If, however, firms execute their investment plans during particular periods, and do so more or less in concert, business cycles will result. In this case, the growth trend appears in the form of a sequence of surges in investment and in output growth. During these surges, growth takes place at a rate in excess of the trend. The trend reasserts itself as a limit to growth in the short run, and investment surges give way to a slump during which growth proceeds at a rate which falls short of the trend.

If the slump is not too acute, prospects for revival will be good. As inventories diminish, pressure for investment in circulating capital revives. Investors consider the advantages of capital formation in anticipation of renewed growth in demand. So long as investors carry the conviction through the slump that revival is inevitable, that conviction, together with the natural workings of the economy, should assure revival. To put this point somewhat differently, the idea of the trend carries through the slump and assures that the lapse in investment will only be temporary. The idea of a trend, then, plays a critical role in assuring that the slump will be self-limiting.

The degree of instability of the economy enters into consideration when we try to assess its ability to support the idea of a long-run trend. If cumulative processes move beyond certain limits, they may disrupt both the ability of the trend to reassert itself and the conviction that it must eventually do so. Thus, for example, if speculative movements in financial markets sufficiently disorganize the Banking System as to significantly impede the flow of finance to firms, the institutional framework for investment breaks down. When the underlying economic institutions (in this case banks) fail, we experience a genuine breakdown in the accumulation process and not merely a pause in the long-run trend. Similar problems arise if the slump is, for whatever reason, sufficiently deep and protracted as to undermine the assumption that it is in the nature of a pause in an on-going process. Under these circumstances, forces working toward the revival of investment face a potentially insurmountable obstacle. As a result, the state of expectations about the future does not support current investment at a rate adequate to bring about a renewed surge of economic growth.

During such periods, the economy loses its capacity to support the idea that agents can rely upon the market for their sustenance. If we allow this idea to depend entirely upon the internal resources of the market taken by itself within the context of minimal institutional support—the classic free market under laissez faire—we subject the confidence of economic agents to serious jeopardy. The market can sustain itself only when its agents carry the conviction that the market will sustain itself, but cumulative processes in the market threaten that conviction and endanger the reproduction of the market.

Government intervention in a private enterprise economy has the purpose of supporting and sustaining the idea that the market is a coherent and reliable entity. To accomplish this purpose, the state must prevent cumulative processes from overstepping boundaries defined by those points at which 1.) basic institutions necessary to the accumulation process are disorganized, and 2.) the conviction on the part of economic agents regarding the future is threatened.

Limits can be placed upon cumulative processes in two different, though not mutually exclusive, ways. First, an institutional framework can be set in place which automatically constrains the movement of the economy. Second, constraints on the economy can be made contingent upon the discretion of the state. The first method follows the logic of the classical approach to the relation of state to economy. It leaves the economy to its own devices, but, in contrast to the classical method, provides a much richer institutional framework capable not only of assuring property rights, but also of narrowing the scope for the exercise of those rights. In this respect, the first method implies a redefinition of property rights.

The second method for limiting cumulative processes is the one we normally identify with the idea of economic policy. The difference between the two methods has to do with the element of discretion and, therefore, with the role of politics. When we use policy to stabilize the economy, the measures taken to restrict fluctuations depend upon the results of a political process.

In this paper, we will focus on the sources of instability within the financial circulation and the relation of financial instability to the disorganization of the accumulation process. We will then consider the two different methods by which the state can attempt to control the financial circulation in order to keep its movements within those limits consistent with the on-going process of capital accumulation and economic development.

2. Instability and Crisis

A private enterprise economy includes a group of individual economic agents who make decisions upon the basis of the expected impact of those decisions on their profit and wealth positions. That impact, in turn, depends upon decisions made by other individuals within that same group, so it follows that economic activity tends to take on a cumulative character. Cumulative processes result when decisions oriented toward enhancing the wealth positions of individuals or the profitability of firms become self-reinforcing. Such cumulative processes assure that the reproduction process of a capitalist economy will tend to be unstable.

For this reason, the growth process of a capitalist economy is never smooth and does not tend to settle into a steady path. This normal instability must, however, be clearly distinguished from the phenomenon of economic crisis. The failure to make this distinction has lent a significant degree of incoherence to certain prominent versions of the Marxian treatment of the capitalist cycle.[1] By confusing instability with crisis, such theories lose track of the specificity of crises and, particularly, their specificity to processes internal to the financial circulation. Indeed, the confusion of instablity with crisis supports the extremely problematic interpretation of crises as real rather than financial phenomena.

Crises of disproportionality and of realization are argued to occur when the structure of demand for output differs from that of supply. During such crises, the movement of physical output among the sectors of the economy is impeded by the lack of coordination between units of production. The idea that imbalance between sectors causes crises clearly places the burden of the explanation on processes internal to the industrial circulation. This method of explanation can also be found justifying the model of steady, or balanced, growth as a way of understanding deviations from the path of balanced growth. These deviations are then identified with fluctuations and crises in such a way as to make it appear that a causal relation holds.

For this theory to carry weight, two assumptions must hold: 1.) the reproduction process of a capitalist economy must be so fragile that it cannot absorb imbalances into its normal functioning; this means that the structure of production and marketing does not incorporate mechanisms (e.g., holding of inventories or excess capacity) capable of dealing with the absence of explicit coordination of private decisions; and 2.) the structure of the economy must be such as to normally encourage or allow fluctuations to proceed beyond limits associated with continuing reproduction. The fragility assumption, with reference to the industrial circulation, plays an important part in those theories which see crises as essentially real phenomena.

As it turns out, however, the industrial circulation does incorporate structural features which, while in no way capable of assuring steady growth, nonetheless limit fluctuations and absorb imbalances. Two particularly important characteristics of the industrial circulation absorb imbalances and limit fluctuations as regards their time dimensions and their amplitude.

First, movements within this sector center on conditions of profitability which involve long-run considerations. When profitability depends upon structural features of the economy (including technology, competition, and demand), the structure of the economy also limits the pursuit of profit. Thus, the classical theory invokes the idea of a competitive process centered around a normal profit rate to establish the coherence of the price system. So long as the idea of normal profit has force, it acts as a limit to investment and pricing decisions and, therefore, as a limit to fluctuations in investment and prices.

Second, the processes of production and of investment in a producing apparatus have a time dimension which, while consistent with fluctuations, differs from the time dimension of a crisis. The rapidity with which decisions are made, their ramifications felt, and new decisions brought into play, which characterizes a crisis, does not allow for the time-consuming processes of investment and production. The term *crisis* connotes a process which happens in a time dimension all its own. Within a crisis, decisions are quickly reinforced or reversed, and they are always made with an eye both to their reversal and to an immediate test of their value.

These two characteristics of the industrial circulation tend to make it an inappropriate locus for the origin of crises. At the same time, the absence of these two conditions make the financial circulation a likely source of the kind of instability associated with crises. Movements within the financial circulation need not center on a calculation of profitability linked to commodity production, nor is the time dimension of the financial circulation limited by the period of production and investment.

As we have suggested, the term *crisis* connotes a process that develops over a short period of time and that is discrete in comparison with processes involving periods of production and investment. Crisis connotes a fundamental disruption of the accumulation process which, in effect, suspends its forward momentum. During the normal cycle of capitalist economy, the future controls the present. In particular, expectations of future demand and profitability control current investment decisions. During a crisis, the future, as regards the processes of production and investment, tends to dissipate, expectations falter, and the present (the crisis) perpetuates itself. The break in the forward movement of economic time suspends the investment process, which depends upon expectations about the future. Instability and crisis, then, differ with respect to their temporal dimensions and, particularly, with respect to their manner of connecting present and future.

Because the business cycle does not depend on a sudden, sharp break in the transition from present to future, it is consistent with the temporal dimension of the industrial circulation. The downswing of the cycle generally involves failure of effective demand, disproportion between sectors, and, in this sense, problems of realization. A downswing need not, however, imply a crisis. Indeed if the two phenomena are logically dependent, it is because a crisis, origininating outside the industrial circulation, can have a significantly disruptive effect on the investment process. In the following sections, we will consider first the role of monetary and financial factors in the business cycle, and then the specific phenomenon of crisis. We will then use this analysis to argue for an institutional rather than policy-oriented conception of the relation of government to economy.

3. Monetary Factors and the Business Cycle

Given that business cycles are generated by forces that tend to produce the bunching of investment in time, monetary factors operate within the cycle through their effect on the financial considerations connected to the timing of investment decisions by the firm. Because investment expenditure involves the purchase of long-lived equipment with a long payoff period, investment expenditure is likely to be larger than the current flow of net profits. Its financing will require the firm to make adjustments in its balance sheet. Such adjustments can be classified into two broad categories: 1.) adjustments associated with internal finance; and 2.) adjustments associated with external finance.

Credit conditions affect investment that is to be internally financed in different ways than they affect investment that is to be externally financed. To simplify the discussion, we assume that the decision to finance internally or externally is not significantly affected by current credit conditions, so that the proportion of planned investment that is to be internally financed can be taken as a given in the following discussion.

In this section, we will examine possible ways in which credit conditions can affect the pace of investment, assuming that the credit system does not become disorganized in the course of the business cycle. In section 4, we will discuss monetary crisis and its effects on the real sector of the economy.

We can describe credit conditions in two ways—by the cost of credit and by the availability of credit. Both are determined by the supply of credit relative to the demand for credit. The supply of credit depends on the quantity of that asset considered to be the standard of liquidity for all of the other assets in the credit system (to be referred to as outside money) and on the liquidity preference of lenders.[2] The demand for credit depends on the pace of investment and the proportion of investment that is to be externally financed. We will consider cost and availability mechanisms in turn.

In the following, we make two assumptions for ease of exposition and analysis. First, we assume that the government determines the rate of growth of the stock of outside money in the economy.[3] Second, we assume that the term structure of interest rates is constant over the cycle so that we can speak simply of *the* rate of interest.

If the stock of outside money is "sticky" relative to the pace of investment, so that it does not change in an accommodating manner in relation to the demand for credit, then interest rates in open credit markets are likely to vary in a counter-cyclical pattern, rising over the boom and falling over the slump, as demand grows faster than supply during the boom and more slowly than supply during the slump. Alternatively, in segments of the credit system where credit flows are mediated by firms (not by open markets) and where price-setting behavior is observed, a counter-cyclical pattern of interest rates will also be observed. To some extent the interest rate charged borrowers in the real sector of the economy will vary counter-cyclically because the cost of lenders' funds secured on the open market rises over the boom and falls over the slump. In addition, we would not expect financial firms to lower interest rates, when the growth of credit demand is strong, in an effort to support the volume of loans in their portfolios. Price-cutting behavior by lenders makes more sense in a recession when loan volume is low because investment expenditure is low.

If the stock of outside money accommodates movements in the demand for credit over the cycle, stability of interest rates over the cycle will result. Monetary factors will be neutral in this case, as the following discussion of the cost factor indicates.

The level of nominal interest-rates relative to past and expected future nominal interest rates is the cost indicator of credit conditions. The relation of current rates to past rates bears on that proportion of planned investment which is to be internally financed, while the relation of current rates to future rates bears on that proportion of planned investment which is to be externally financed.[4]

The internal finance of investment requires that financial assets purchased in the past be sold for current purchasing power. The terms of these sales depend on conditions in the secondary debt market. If interest rates are high (low) relative to past levels, financing investment may engender large capital losses (gains), inducing firms to postpone (bring forward) their planned investment.

The external finance of investment requires that new financial assets be sold for current purchasing power at a price inversely related to the rate of interest. If interest rates are high (low) relative to expected future levels, firms may be induced to postpone (bring forward) planned investment in order to avoid (take the opportunity to) committing themselves to high (low) nominal interest payments.[5] Both of these interest-rate mechanisms will be stronger, the longer the term to maturity of the assets to be liquidated or the debt to be floated. If short-term assets are to be liquidated or issued, the capital losses (gains) will be correspondingly smaller and the commitment to make high interest payments will be over a shorter time period, leaving the firm the option of refinancing at lower interest rates, either short-term or long-term.

The price of financial assets can affect the pace of investment, not only through the cost of credit, but also because of the potential for profit making from investing in the financial circulation instead of the real circulation. When interest rates are high relative to expected future rates (when asset prices are expected to rise), speculative capital gains can be secured by purchasing financial assets instead of real assets.

If nominal interest rates move counter-cyclically, then the level of nominal interest rates and the level of nominal net profits are positively correlated. This positive correlation may weaken the effectiveness of the cost mechanism. When current flows of net profits are large, they can be used to finance current investment, requiring that fewer financial assets be liquidated (with possibly large capital losses) and that fewer new debts be issued (at high interest rates). Since current profits are received in money, no capital losses are suffered from using increments to financial assets accruing from current sales to finance current investment.

Cost-of-credit conditions that induce firms to postpone investment during a boom can offset the bunching phenomenon and moderate the expansion phase of the cycle, to the extent that investment spending is postponed by some firms. Similarly, credit conditions that induce firms to initiate investment during a slump, instead of waiting to invest in the future, have a stabilizing influence on the magnitude of the business cycle. However, monetary factors must be sufficiently strong in either the boom or the slump as to dominate real factors in order to have a stabilizing effect on the cycle.

Monetary factors working through the availability of credit affect primarily that portion of planned investment which is to be externally financed and which cannot be internally financed in the event that credit cannot be secured. If the demand for credit is highly interest inelastic, then the cost-of-credit mechanism will have very little effect on the pace of investment. If firms are unable to secure their desired level of credit at any price, then they face a supply-of-finance constraint that causes investment to be below desired levels. The availability mechanism can limit actual investment during a boom, stabilizing cyclical fluctuations or, during a slump, prolonging the recession and causing the fall in investment to be lower than it would be in the absence of the finance constraint.

The availability mechanism works as an inhibiting force or as a facilitating force. Its potential potency is greater as an inhibiting force than as a facilitating force; while the absence of the requisite amount of finance will impede firms from carrying out their planned level of investment, the existence of the requisite amount of finance simply allows them to carry out a planned level of investment (it does not cause actual investment to exceed planned investment).[6]

The availability argument rests on the idea that the credit system has a finite capacity, at a given time, and that once full utilization of that capacity is reached, the elasticity of the supply of credit is zero. This raises the question of whether the postulate of a zero elasticity of supply of credit in a capitalist economy, in which finance capital is privately owned, is meaningful.

The capacity of the credit system is determined by the quantity of outside money in the economy and the liquidity preference of lenders. Outside money is the financial asset into which all other financial assets are convertible, either directly or indirectly. Inside money, issued by banks, is convertible into outside money, while nonmonetary assets are convertible into inside money, either at maturation (if they are bilateral assets, that is, without secondary markets) or at a time determined by the will of the holder of the asset (if they are market assets, with secondary markets). Issuers of inside money, then, must be concerned with the relationship between their liabilities, in the form of inside money, and their assets, in the form of outside money. Issuers of nonmonetary assets must be concerned with the relationship between their liabilities, in the form of nonmonetary assets, and their assets, in the form of inside money. These relationships capture the workings of liquidity preference in the economy.

The amount of financial intermediation which a given stock of outside money can support, then, depends on the extent to which banks are willing, and able, to lever their balance sheets in relation to their stocks of outside money and on the extent to which issuers of nonmonetary liabilities are willing, and able, to lever their balance sheets in relation to their stocks of inside money. The ability to lever depends on the demand conditions for the liabilities issued by financial firms, by banks and nonbanks alike, and by nonfinancial firms. The capacity of the credit system, with a given amount of outside money in the system, is reached once financial and nonfinancial firms alike have reached their debt limits, determined both internally to the firm and externally by the firm's potential creditors.

If the state restricts the supply of outside money (relative to the demand for credit) to the credit system, the accommodation of a growing demand for credit will require financial firms and nonfinancial lenders to become more levered in relation to outside money and inside money. The intensity of the use of outside money and inside money as credit bases will increase as rising interest rates induce the substitution of nonmonetary assets for money.[7]

The interest elasticity of the demand for money determines the size of the rise in interest rates on money substitutes required to induce holders of money to change the composition of their liquid assets. Financial firms do not take the interest elasticity of money demand as an immutable given, however. By devising new kinds of financial instruments with features that are highly money-like from the point of view of the individual wealthholder, financial firms can increase the interest elasticity of money demand and so reduce the costs of expanding their assets. The quantity of money required by the individual firm or household for transactions purposes places an upper limit on the reduction of money balances and thus on the velocity of money and on the intensity of use of the monetary base. Furthermore, once liquidity is reduced to this minimum level, concerns about the size of precautionary buffer stocks of money relative to nonmonetary assets may take hold, which make the demand for money absolutely interest inelastic (that is, dominated by nonprice factors).

Limits to the intensity of use of the credit base may be reached before the point where the stock of inside money is fully utilized in current account transactions. Potential holders of financial assets may become concerned about the leverage of the issuers of assets and prefer to hold increments to their wealth in the form of money. That is, liquidity preference may cause the demand for money to become interest inelastic before the stock of inside money is fully utilized in current account transactions. This will limit the growth of credit in the economy.

If concern with liquidity translates itself into efforts by wealthholders not only to increase the proportion of increments to their financial wealth in the form of money, but also to increase the proportion of their entire stocks of wealth that takes the form of money, this will have effects not only on increments to the supply of credit, but also on the total amount of financial intermediation in the economy. In such cases, where liquidity preference is particularly strong, cumulative processes may develop.

Movement out of nonmonetary financial assets into money by a subset of wealthholders has a depressing effect on the level of financial asset prices and on the monetary value of the financial assets owned by the other wealthholders in the economy. As these wealthholders seek to preserve the value of their financial wealth by selling nonmonetary financial assets for money, the price of financial assets falls further. In such episodes, the actions taken by individual wealthholders on the basis of expected deflation of financial asset prices have the aggregate effect of actually deflating financial asset prices. To the degree that the actual deflation of financial asset prices feeds back into expected future prices, a cumulative process of financial asset deflation results. A "shock" to the financial market, instead of triggering processes that restore the prevailing level of financial asset prices, triggers a cumulative process that reinforces the initial direction of movement of asset prices.

However, if the state is committed to preserving the coherence of the financial structure, and the public understands this to be a fact fundamental to the credit system, the liquidity-preference limit to increasing the intensity of use of the stock of money (inside and outside) may never be reached, and cumulative processes of asset price deflation may never develop. As financial firms become more and more levered, any suggestion that holders of nonmonetary assets may start to move en masse out of such assets and into money will require the state to inject outside money into the system in order to reduce the leverage of financial firms and forestall widespread shifts in the structure of demand for financial assets. As it does so, the potential capacity of the credit system expands, and the prior expansion of the credit system by the private sector is validated.

As long as the state stands committed to preventing monetary crises, then, it is unlikely that the capacity limit of the credit system will ever be reached. This bypasses the possibility of a significant availability mechanism. However, the availability doctrine comes into its own with a vengeance once we suspend the assumption that the state is committed to preserving the coherence of the financial system.

4. Monetary Crisis

A monetary crisis occurs when there is a widespread collapse in the values of the financial assets which comprise the credit system. This collapse is the result of a cumulative process of asset price deflation, described in the previous section. In this section, we will investigate this process more closely, starting from a discussion of the basic properties of financial assets and of the system in which they are located.

Financial assets have special properties which make widespread collapse of their values possible. Because they are nonproduced commodities, the complex of factors that produce stability in the prices of produced commodities are absent. This is due to certain peculiarities of financial markets, vis-à-vis commodity markets, on the side of both demand and supply. These peculiarities stem from the fact that financial markets clear in stock terms. On the side of demand, this means that changes in the demand for a particular financial asset affect not just increments to the stock of that asset (as it would in the case of a produced commodity, whose market clears in flow terms), but the entire outstanding stock of that asset. Large changes in demand, then, can occur over very short periods of time.

In markets for produced commodities, a fall in demand or in the rate of growth of demand for a particular commodity occurs gradually. As demand contracts, so does the amount of utilized productive capacity in that particular market. The quantity response on the supply side of the market limits the extent of price adjustment. In financial markets the supply in terms of the number of units of the asset cannot fall when demand falls, so all of the adjustment occurs as a fall in its price.

While the principle of normal profit delimits the possible range of movement of the prices of produced commodities, no such principle operates in financial markets. Keynes developed the term *convention* to capture the process of determination of normal price in financial markets. For Keynes, the convention ensured that the market valuation of financial claims "is uniquely correct in relation to our existing knowledge of the facts which will influence the yield of the investment, and that it will only change in proportion to changes in this knowledge."[8] As long as the convention holds, fluctuations in asset prices will be limited by fluctuations in the productivity of capital structures, as determined in commodity markets. However, as security markets develop, Keynes argues, they acquire properties which tend to undermine the convention. As the convention breaks down, the possibility for large fluctuations in financial asset prices develops.

Once asset price determination is severed from the productivity of real capital assets, expectations of what average opinion expects the average opinion to be take over. In such a market, a cumulative process can develop in which individual wealthholders expect prices to rise, and believe that other wealthholders will continue to expect prices to rise, allowing speculative gains to be secured as asset prices in fact rise due to strong monetary demand for financial assets.[9]

Because of the short time dimension of financial asset markets, which is tied to the mechanism of stock adjustment in those markets, expectations can be confirmed or negated shortly following the decision which they motivated. In a speculative episode, the excess of actual gains over expected gains can fuel the inflation of asset prices, while in an episode of collapse of asset values, the excess of actual losses over expected losses can reinforce the deflationary process. This is in sharp distinction to commodity markets, in which the results of a decision to invest in a real capital asset are known only over a long time period that encompasses a number of periods of production and sale of commodities. The absence of a firm foundation for normal prices in security markets creates the possibility of large fluctuations in the prices of individual securities. The upper limit to asset prices depends on how long such an expectational process can be sustained. Similarly, the lower limit to financial asset prices can be quite low relative to a previous peak, depending on the strength of extrapolative expectations during the downward movement of asset prices.

The credit system can be seen as a pyramid of financial assets. Within this pyramid, the stock of inside money is a multiple of the stock of outside money; otherwise, the amount of intermediation which the system is capable of performing would be limited to the value of the stock of outside money. Similarly, the stock of nonmonetary inside assets is a multiple of the stock of inside money in the economy. Secondary asset markets allow large changes in the demand for nonmonetary inside assets, counterposed to a fixed supply, to engender either changes in relative prices (as when demand increases for one nonmonetary asset while decreasing for another) or changes in the price level of financial assets (as when demand increases for money while decreasing for nonmonetary assets).

Changes in liquidity preference engender fluctuations in the value of financial wealth. In the case where liquidity preference is low and falling, the demand for nonmonetary inside assets increases while their supply is relatively fixed. As the monetary value of financial assets rises, the proportion of money in the total stock of financial wealth falls. Similarly, where liquidity preference is strong, the monetary value of financial assets falls as wealthholders sell nonmonetary financial assets for money. The proportion of money in the total stock of financial wealth rises.

Instability in the financial markets, which is the other side of an unstable speculative demand for money, can give way to crisis. Crisis is rooted in the basic structural feature of the credit system that not all of the nonmonetary assets can be converted into inside money without a severe deflation of the values of those assets. Likewise, not all of the inside money can be converted into outside money at a given time without a destruction of a portion of the stock of inside money. (Since inside money exchanges against outside money at par, there is no price that can change to adjust the value of inside money.) The stability of financial asset values rests on an orderly rate of conversion of inside nonmonetary assets into inside money and of inside money into outside money.

Inside nonmonetary assets can be converted into inside money for the system of wealthholders through the scheduled payment of interest and principle or, for the individual wealthholder, through the sale of an asset on the secondary debt market. Timely conversions of the first kind depend largely on actual income flows relative to income flows projected at the date when the debt was issued. Conversions of the second kind depend on demand conditions in the secondary debt market. Where demand is highly price elastic, conversions can be made with a small reduction in price; where demand is price inelastic, conversions can only be made by accepting a large reduction in price. In the extreme case of a financial crisis, the concern for liqudiity becomes predominant so that conversions become impossible, in which case the current monetary value of financial assets falls to zero. Conversions become impossible when there is pessimistic sentiment about the value of financial assets in the immediate future throughout the community of wealthholders.

Unanimous pessimistic sentiment can develop after periods of speculation in which asset prices rise to levels far in excess of their normal levels, as determined by a market consensus based on a convention which has broken down. Once financial markets reach this point, there is nowhere for asset prices to go but down, and the possible deflation of asset prices, and associated capital losses, becomes large.

Such a state may originate in one particular subset of markets and then spread to other financial markets. The propogation of the collapse of asset values works through interconnected balance sheets. Inside assets are assets which represent debts of units in the private sector. Debt-credit relations among units in the private sector create links between balance sheets of economic units. The propogation mechanism rests on the financial interdependence among economic units, in which units provide other units with the means of financing deficits and are provided with a means of expanding wealth without fixing it into a particular commodity form.

There are several kinds of propogation processes which can cause the collapse of asset values to become generalized throughout the credit system. Holders of the assets in which the process originated suffer capital losses. To the extent that these assets were to be liquidated in order to meet maturing liabilities, either firms may default on their liabilities or firms may sell other financial assets in order to secure the necessary money to service their debt, initiating a process of price deflation in those markets. If assets are defaulted on, the interruption of payments on the debt can undermine the ability of creditors to fulfill their own debt contracts on a timely basis, leading them to make similar adjustments, which have an impact upon other asset markets.[10]

Because of the mechanism of stock adjustment in financial markets, the propogation process can be quite rapid. Individual wealthholders can seek to change the composition of their entire stock of financial assets within a very short time period. As a result, very large changes in asset prices can occur over very short time periods. For crises to be discrete events, they must originate in such markets.

As wealthholders as a group seek to become more liquid and sell financial assets for money in order to do so, this will bring about the widespread devaluation of nonmonetary financial assets, in the absence of some source of support for the effective (monetary) demand for financial assets originating outside the group of private wealthholders. If the quantity of money is fixed throughout this process, then prices of nonmonetary financial assets must fall until money and nonmonetary financial assets are in the desired proportion at the level of the economy as a whole. The financial wealth of each individual unit, which sought to change only its composition and not its size, shrinks accordingly.

A widespread collapse of asset values affects the real sector in two ways. First, holders of financial assets in the real sector of the economy suffer losses in the value of their financial wealth. While their real wealth purchased in the past remains intact, their pool of purchasing power over newly producible real wealth has shrunk (assuming that commodity price formation is independent of the forces that generated deflation of financial asset prices). This exerts a financial constraint on aggregate demand and increases the percentage of planned investment that is to be externally financed. This constraint could be overcome through growth in credit, but growth in credit will be limited so long as the preference for the most liquid asset remains strong.

The second effect works through the supply of credit. As long as liquidity preference remains strong, potential lenders will be reluctant to exchange nonmonetary financial assets for money, so that the ratio of nonmonetary financial assets to money in the system as a whole will remain low, relative to levels attained prior to the crisis. In effect, the monetary crisis, through its effect on confidence and liquidity preference, causes the capacity of the credit system to shrink, although the stock of outside money has not fallen. The level of investment planned by firms may not be attained if it is associated with a demand for credit that exceeds the capacity of the credit system.

The monetary crisis affects the business cycle through inhibiting the finance of planned investment, causing actual investment to fall short of planned investment. This may abort a cyclical expansion or deepen and prolong an on-going recession. The first effect of a monetary crisis mentioned, the fall in the value of financial wealth, also has implications for the long-run process of capital accumulation.

The long-run process of capital accumulation involves the use of the existing capital stock as a basis for the formation and further accumulation of capital. Financial assets play a special role in this process. Profits generated from capital formed in the past add to the firm's stock of finance available for the funding of current or future additions to its capital stock. Financial assets, then, carry value generated by capital formed in the past into the present and future.

Monetary crisis interferes with the transitional work of financial assets. Performance of this transitional work requires that the purchasing power of financial assets over produced commodities be somewhat stable over the lifetime of the asset. A financial asset's purchasing power depends on the terms of its conversion into money at the time purchasing power is needed and on the terms of the conversion of money into produced commodities. During a monetary crisis, financial assets are devalued in terms of money. Unless commodity prices have deflated by as much as the devaluation of financial asset prices, a given stock of financial assets yields to its owners reduced purchasing power over commodities. The existing capital stock becomes a less adequate basis for further capital expansion, not because of a change in the productive potential of the existing capital stock, but because of the devaluation of the claims to the wealth generated by that capital stock.

Because of the damage that monetary crisis inflicts on the state of confidence, and because confidence is a necessary requirement of a functioning credit system, the reconstitution of the credit system after a crisis may require a long time. In the interim, external finance is apt to be inadequate to fill the gap in total financing needs created by the devaluation of the existing stock of financial assets. When monetary crisis occurs, it prolongs the interruption of the growth process by reducing the ex post profitability of the existing capital stock and by disorganizing the supply side of the credit system.

5. Monetary Structure and Monetary Policy

Monetary policy that seeks to affect credit conditions addresses itself to the stabilization of the business cycle. Since credit conditions are only one of a number of factors which affect the firm's timing of investment decisions, the conduct of monetary policy is often a frustrating venture; it is not unusual to find monetary authorities expressing dismay that investment spending remains strong in spite of tight credit and that it remains weak in spite of easy credit. Where the monetary factor really comes into its own is when monetary crisis threatens.

The state has two alternative methods for dealing with the problem of monetary crisis. One method is to intervene in financial markets once crisis conditions start to develop. The crisis can be averted by providing outside money to the credit system at points of tension within it, where the value of assets is being undermined. Such acts are discretionary in the sense that they are directed to a particular segment of the credit system at a particular point in time and in the sense that the state could decide not to perform them. These acts of intervention in financial markets are the outcome of a process of policy making.

A second method is to change the organization of financial markets in such a way that precludes the development of crisis conditions. By reorganizing financial markets with a view to stabilizing them, the state achieves its objectives automatically—that is, without making policy decisions. In reorganizing the financial markets, however, the state redefines the range of proper uses of wealth in a way that limits wealth seeking through financial speculation.

Margin requirements that define the maximum proportion of a prospective purchase of a financial asset that can be borrowed are one example of a legislative change designed to limit speculation. This legislation gives the state the authority to establish the cash requirements of financial investment. This would, hypothetically, limit the volume of transactions in the secondary asset markets by imposing a finance constraint, and so contain speculation. A financial system that includes regulations such as margin requirements is structurally more stable than a system without them. Once in place, such regulations change the workings of financial markets by removing from them potential sources of instability. This kind of stabilization works automatically, since it does not require a policy decision by the state to do its work.

The second method is superior to the first insofar as the goal of stabilizing the financial system is concerned. As long as stabilization is the result of a discretionary policy decision, the possibility that the state will decide not to intervene in a stabilizing manner persists. This has a destabilizing effect on financial markets since it widens the possible range of movement of asset prices. As wealthholders perceive the financial markets to be potentially unstable, they participate in those markets in a way that creates an unstable financial structure. Reorganization of the financial markets can create a new regime in which belief in the persistence of normal prices produces asset price stability. The belief in normal prices, far from being subjectively determined by a psychological convention, would be objectively determined by market practices which preclude speculation.

While the state has made changes in the organization of the financial system with a view to stabilizing the financial system, these changes have evolved in response to an actual or a potential monetary crisis. As the financial markets develop, however, the locus of structural weakness created by speculation changes, so that the legislation that is in place in order to contain speculation is out-of-date.[11]

As a result, crisis conditions are allowed to develop, requiring the state to act in a crisis-averting manner. Because the state is hesitant to institute changes in financial structure that would prevent crisis, it limits itself to conducting policy within the confines of a potentially unstable financial structure.

6. Conclusion

The instability of a private enterprise economy results not simply from the fact that social outcomes depend upon decisions made by individual property owners without explicit coordination, but from the specific objectives which drive those property owners. Instability originates in the pursuit of gain through the use of wealth as capital. The objective of wealth expansion tends to proceed without limit. When the producing and marketing structure, and especially its innate capacity to generate profit, fails to limit the process of value expansion, instability can give birth to crisis. This is precisely the problem which arises within the financial circulation. The use of capital for speculative purposes frees the value of ownership claims over capital from constraints associated with production and with the calculation of profit from the production and sale of commodities. For this reason, the financial circulation lacks the internal ordering principle which, within the industrial circulation, lends coherence to a system of private, independent, agents.

The classical economists saw in competition a force which lends coherence to the system of private property and pursuit of private interest. Because of competition, the system of property owners acting upon the basis of separate and conflicting interests had a coherence when taken as a whole. But, in order for competition to act as an ordering force, it must presuppose certain determinate limits which, for classical political economy, were given outside of the competitive process. The idea of average profit (rooted in the idea of the subsistence wage) provided such a limit. In more modern versions of the classical theory (generally rooted in the work of Alfred Marshall), the idea of normal profit sets upper and lower limits to investment, output, and price determination.

Whether or not we accept the ideas of normal and average profitability, we can still see profit as a relevant limit to movements within the industrial circulation. In an earlier section, we emphasized the link between profit, the structure of production and marketing, and the temporal framework of profit making as limits to instability within the industrial circulation. We then demonstrated how the absence of such limits within the financial circulation made possible the transition from instability to crisis.

The more serious instability of the financial circulation need not be a matter of concern so long as it leaves the industrial circulation intact. As we have seen, however, this need not be the case, and indeed when the disorganization of the financial circulation is sufficiently severe, it cannot but lead to a significant disruption of the accumulation process. In such cases, the pursuit of private gain threatens the system within which that pursuit takes place. The disorganization of the financial circulation undermines the investment process and, therefore, the conditions of profit making within the industrial circulation. These conditions of profitability are also necessary conditions for the financial circulation, which is a circulation of claims to shares in the profit produced by industry. Thus, the pursuit of private gain in the financial sector, if not limited, can be self-destructive.

Control over the financial circulation is a way of asserting the claims of the system of individual pursuit of private gain over the individual pursuit of private gain. This conclusion is important because it establishes the first principled basis for government intervention within a private enterprise economy. This basis for intervention is consistent with the underlying principles of private enterprise. The government limits the exercise of property rights, in this case use of property for speculative purposes, in order to preserve the system of property relations.

If we think of government intervention as setting limits to the use of property in order to preserve the system of property ownership, then we can identify two methods of accomplishing this end. First, the government can directly limit the use of property by, in effect, altering the legal definition of and limits to property right. Second, the government can encourge economic agents to use their property in ways which tend to encourage stability, without directly limiting the discretion which individuals have over the use of their property.

The second method of intervention is the one we normally associate with the idea of policy. When, for example, the government attempts to assure that the values of securities remain within certain limits by supporting their prices through buying and selling, the government does not directly tamper with the logic of the market. Instead, it fully accepts the organization of the market, but attempts indirectly to stimulate a certain quantitative outcome, one consistent with stable valuation.

In this case, the government acts as one more private agent pursuing its own ends within a system of independent property owners. The difference between the state and other particular agents is that, while other agents pursue private gain, the government pursues stability. Still, it does so as a particular property owner.

This result ties in well with the idea that policy making has an intrinsically discretionary aspect. Since the state adopts the persona, so to speak, of an individual property owner, it acts in pursuit of interests which appear in a form appropriate to a particular agent. This means that the state acts with the discretion of an economic agent. In effect, the state pursues a public purpose—stabilization as a means of assuring the reproduction of the property system—by acting as one among a system of private agents pursuing particular ends within a structure of their own making. Clearly the state has advantages associated with size, but these advantages are, appropriately, purely quantitative. Within the financial system, they are no different in kind from those of the larger financial institutions.

Why should the state, which is not after all a private agent, limit itself to pursuing the public interest in that guise? In other words, why should the state limit itself to contingent policy-making, when it has the authority to alter the institutional framework of the property system in such a way as to assure that, regardless of any particular action undertaken by particular agents including itself, the reproduction of the property system will proceed within normal bounds?

Two answers to this question help to clarify the idea of policy-making. First, going beyond the limits of discretionary policy-making action, as outlined above, requires redefining the limits of property rights, and this opens up the fundamental question concerning the proper and necessary limits to the property system itself. Second, in the absence of agreement (either voluntary or otherwise) concerning these limits, steps taken to curb the instability of the market are contingent upon the outcome of a political process. The discretionary element reflects the unwillingness of the polity to clearly articulate the limiting framework of the market system.

Because of this, the idea of policy-making expresses a fundamental contradiction within the structure of a private enterprise economy. The idea of private enterprise arises on the basis of the principle of minimal limitation of the exercise of property rights. But when the workings of an economy based upon maximum discretion in the ownership and use of property leads naturally to its own disorganization, as suggested above, modification is required in the organization of the property system. When such modifications conflict with the fundamental idea which motivates the organization of the economy, those modifications must present themselves in a form apparently consistent with that idea. In this case, the pursuit of a principle, stable reproduction, not built into a private enterprise economy, must be done in a way which makes it appear as part of the logic of such an economy. This happens when the state acts as a private agent in pursuit of the public interest. And this has the effect of displacing the underlying contradiction in the workings of the economy from the economy itself to the debate over policies to be pursued under the framework of a given system of property rights and economic institutions.

The issue which underlies macropolicy debate is that of the nature and limits of the property system (or economy). Because the idea of private property carries with it the implication that use of property is subject to the discretion of its owners, the property system is intrinsically outside of the direct control of the state. Within the defined limits of the property system, the state treats that system as an external entity with its own internal laws. Like the laws of nature, economic laws can be manipulated but not altered. While the state cannot alter economic laws, it can redefine the limits within which those laws operate. When it does so, it no longer requires policy to achieve its ends. When it does not, the idea of policy becomes relevant. This means that the enterprise of policy-making embodies a contradiction when the ends pursued through policy conflict with the defined limits of the property system.

Notes

1. The discussion in the text refers to the literature on economic crisis viewed narrowly. Within Marxist literature, there is also a broader notion of systemic crisis which has to do with the long-run process of capitalist development. Our criticism of the Marxist theory is not meant to apply to this broader idea.

2. This definition of outside money is different from that developed by Gurley and Shaw (1960), which is the conventional definition used in the literature on monetary theory and policy. The property of outside money stressed by Gurley and Shaw is that it is not the liability of a private economic unit and it is not issued against the liability of a private economic unit. The property of outside money stressed in this paper is that, in distinction to inside money and inside nonmonetary assets, it is not redeemable into any other asset. This makes it the ultimate standard of liquidity.

3. This does not necessarily mean, however, that the rate of growth of outside money is purely exogenous with respect to the rate of growth of credit demand; as Kaldor (1980 pp. 17–18) argues, it may depend on the level of activity in the private sector.

4. In an inflationary economy, past expected, current actual, and expected future changes in the price level must also be considered, assuming that the inflation premium contained in nominal interest rates does not necessarily correspond either to 1.) the individual agent's expectations, or to 2.) the actual rate of inflation, over the pertinent time horizon. If the inflation premium contained in nominal interest rates is different from the borrower's expected rate of inflation, the perceived real cost of borrowing to the firm will differ from the real cost of borrowing as embodied in market nominal interest rates. If the inflation premium contained in nominal rates corresponds to the actual rate of inflation (the monetarist assumption), the argument can be posed in terms of real interest rates as they are embodied in nominal interest rates.

5. If the interest rate is constant over the business cycle, then past interest rate equals the current interest rate, and the current interest rate equals the expected future interest rates. In this case, the cost mechanism would not operate.

6. See Hicks (1979, pp. 94–95).

7. Within this process, credit rationing may occur as lenders restrict the availability of credit to marginal firms while making credit available to prime borrowers. This would increase the quality of their assets while their leverage is increasing and so reduce the risk associated with rising leverage.

8. See J. M. Keynes (1936, p. 152).

9. An increase in the speculative demand for nonmonetary financial assets is the other side of a decrease in the speculative demand for money.

10. Minsky (1982, p. 35) describes this liquidation of assets as position-making.
11. See Minsky (1982, pp. 34–36).

References

Gurley, J. and Shaw, E. 1960. *Money in a Theory of Finance*. Washington, D.C., The Brookings Institute.

Hicks, J. 1979. *Causality in Economics*. Oxford, Basil Blackwell.

Kaldor, N. 1980. *Origins of the New Monetarism*. Cardiff, University College Press.

Keynes, J. M. 1936. *The General Theory of Employment, Interest and Money*. New York, Harcourt, Brace and World.

Minsky, H. 1982. The Financial-Instability Hypothesis: Capitalist Processes and the Behavior of the Economy. In: Charles Kindleberger and Jean-Pierre Laffargue (eds.), *Financial Crises: Theory, History, and Policy*. Cambridge, Cambridge University Press.

6 THE CONTEMPORARY SIGNIFICANCE OF BARAN AND SWEEZY'S NOTION OF MONOPOLISTIC CAPITALISM

Joseph Halevi

1. An Overview

This essay will discuss the main contributions of Paul Baran, Paul Sweezy, and Harry Magdoff in the light of, and in relation to, modern macroeconomic analysis. The focus of the paper is therefore on their interpretations of the dynamics of capitalism. These interpretations, while using concepts which can be found in the main body of macroeconomic theory, are cast in an altogether different framework. The extensive use these authors make of Keynesian notions is not aimed at identifying full-employment conditions consistent with equilibrium in the product market, labor market, and money market so as then to proceed to derive the right mix of fiscal and monetary policies. The *fragestellung* of the *Monthly Review* group does not allow for the transformation of economic concepts into a set of levers to tinker with, in order to achieve results defined independently of the modus operandi of the economic system under scrutiny. If we were to limit ourselves to "tinkering theory," there would be no room for contributions like those of the authors we have elected to discuss. Indeed, a Marxist would have nothing to add, for instance, to Frank Hahn's critique of Monetarism based exclusively on the obvious observation that monetarists arbitrarily extend to the "real world" the postulates of General Equilibrium and omit the very restrictive conditions by which competitive equilibria can be obtained (Hahn, 1980; 1981).

The description and the analysis of the modus operandi of contemporary capitalism prior to any policy considerations is at the center of the works of Baran, Magdoff, and Sweezy. The emphasis that in recent times the editors of *Monthly Review* (Magdoff and Sweezy) have been putting on Keynes as a critic of capitalism derives from the view that in Keynes there exists a relationship between the absence in a capitalist economy of a built-in tendency to full employment and the need for radical social reforms necessary to maintain full employment. According to the editors of *Monthly Review* (*MR*), many Keynesians vulgarized Keynes's work "to the point of turning Keynesianism into a cure-all for the capitalist business cycle"; yet contrary to the establishment economists, Keynes "knew that there were real and deadly serious problems to be dealt with and he was not afraid to tackle them" (*MR*, 1983a, p. 11).

Magdoff's and Sweezy's reference to Keynes's willingness to contemplate far-reaching reforms aimed at the elimination of incomes out of capital and wealth concerns the last chapter of the *General Theory*, which deals with the social philosophy influencing the work itself. To this chapter, one should add chapter 16, where Keynes discusses the question of how it would be impossible to maintain full employment in a mature economy with abundant capital goods, unless conditions were created for investment to be carried out even at an almost zero rate of profit (marginal efficiency). The obliteration of the rentier capitalist is seen, in chapter 16, as a sine qua non for obtaining a monetary economy in which the rate of interest could be set so low, if not at negative values, as to compel capitalists to undertake investment activities at a minimal rate of profit.[1] It can be safely argued that in Keynes's view the transition to a world without finance capital involves a gradual process of changes in class relations in the material as well as intellectual sphere—changes bound to affect the long-run development of the system. These are problems that cannot become the subjects of technocratic exercises in a static framework.

Magdoff and Sweezy make the point that "Keynes's great achievement was now seen not as a highly original contribution to the understanding of capitalism's basic modus operandi but as the invention of a set of clever recipes to counteract the ups and downs of the business cycle" (*MR*, 1983a, p. 7). To strengthen their point let us mention a paper by Tobin and Brainard which, on its face value, comes close to the analysis developed in chapter 16 of the *General Theory* (Tobin and Brainard, 1963). Using a static neoclassical model, where in equilibrium the rate of return on capital is equal to its marginal productivity, Tobin and Brainard put forward the view that monetary controls which lower the rate of return on capital are expansionary, while those raising it are deflationary. A list of possible regimes accompanies the given proposition. Any reader of the paper is immediately led to think that what matters is the appropriate recipe and not what might cause enterprise to become—to use Keynes's words—"the bubble on a whirlpool of speculation." Nor is the reader induced to ask any questions as to whether and why in a laissez-faire capitalist system, liquid investment markets have a strong tendency to arise. This liquidity of investment markets is in Keynes strongly associated with a system of ownership relations in which ways to hold savings other than for the purchase of investment goods are open to wealthowners. Only if markets are so organized as to make capital assets easily transformable into money, can the prospect of purchasing a capital asset (capital goods) be rendered attractive vis-à-vis the alternative ways (hoarding and/or lending). In short, casting analytical arguments in terms of policy options has the effect of erasing the critical approach contained in the *General Theory* and of rendering irrelevant all the arguments about the elimination of income out of accumulated wealth and about the logical necessity of the socialization of investment.

The role ascribed to Keynes of a critical bourgeois thinker, or of a disinterested inquirer, by the editors of *MR* precludes any reconciliation with the textbook version of Keynesian economics. In a very concrete sense the Marxian foundations of the *MR* approach help understand the issues raised by Keynes. One important aspect of their approach is their emphasis on the distinction between the factors governing the demand for real capital from the supply of money capital. In the writings of Magdoff and Sweezy are to be found a conceptual and factual criticism of the view, so common among American economists, that the stagnationist tendencies of the last decade are due to a low saving ratio and, consequently, to a shortage of capital (Magdoff and Sweezy, 1977, pp. 91–110; Magdoff and Sweezy, 1981, ch. 18).

Their critique combines Marx's distinction between money capital and commodity capital with Keynes's causation whereby investment determines saving. Money capital, they argue, can be plentiful (the interest rate being very low), and investment demand can at the same time be extremely low. As history has shown, this was the case of the Depression and stagnation of the 1930s, when from the standpoint of capitalist finance there was no shortage of money capital but there were no significant investment opportunities in sight. By the same token growing unused capacity is not incompatible with shortage of money capital represented by relatively high interest rates. Both phenomena have nothing to do with the level of savings. Idle plant and machinery mean that investment can expand only if effective demand, at any given interest rate, increases sufficiently to reactivate a significant proportion of unutilized equipment. The expansion of investment will automatically generate the necessary savings. But the possibility of cheap money capital in a prolonged depression and of dear money capital amidst growing stagnation reflect the evolution of the contradictory relation between real capital accumulation and capitalist finance. Hence a quick collapse of the level of effective demand, accompanied by a price deflation as was the case in 1929–1932, is likely to produce a cheap money situation of the kind envisaged by Marx in the third volume of *Capital*. By contrast, a progressive slide into stagnation, in which it becomes possible to attempt to maintain the flow of profits by means of inflation and debt expansion, is likely to produce the opposite result.

The longer-view approach taken by Baran, Sweezy, and Magdoff compels application of analytical thinking to a concrete subject matter: the historical development of capitalism. In this context, then, the authors' basic acceptance of Keynes's point that, in general, investment is not at the level necessary to employ existing productive forces, is absorbed into a framework in which the increasing difficulties in finding investment outlets are linked to the stagnationist orientation of monopolistic capitalism. Moreover, the consolidation of monopoly capital is not seen independently of the role of public expenditure (Baran, 1973), nor is it seen separately from the multiplication of financial instruments and institutions, which, far from being viewed as factors increasing the allocative efficiency of financial markets, are considered conducive to the formation of liquid investment markets, which make "the capital development of a country [to become] the by-product of the activities of a casino . . . " (Keynes, 1936, p. 159).

In the Baran-Sweezy-Magdoff conception, monopoly capital signals that stage of development where capitalism, once progressive, has become retrograde due to its immanent inability to realize the potential surplus output of the economy. Hence the growing tendencies towards unproductive, but not necessarily socially useful, activities, including the hypertrophic development of the financial superstructure. These are forms and an expression of the slackening of accumulation which enters in contradiction with the valorization of capital. Analytically we are no longer on Keynes's plane but, rather, on the line of inquiry followed by Michal Kalecki and Josef Steindl. It was Kalecki who pointed out that excess capacity is a dominant feature of oligopolistic economies. Steindl, while proceeding from Kalecki, has in turn argued that the long-run decline in capital accumulation in the United States, which eventually materialized in the Great Depression, stemmed from the strengthening of profit margins at the turn of the century, a period regarded as the beginning of what Schumpeter called Trustified Capitalism[2] (Steindl,

1976). Perhaps one of the most interesting, albeit neglected, observations made by Steindl concerns the relation between the effect of oligopolies on accumulation and the rise of joint stock finance. The problem as discussed by Steindl will be analysed in a later section of this paper. It suffices to remark here that Steindl's theme is central to the argument of *MR* aimed at showing how continuing stagnation fuels the multiplication of financial instruments.

When monopoly capital is seen as the core of the capitalist economy and when the core is (correctly) viewed as constituted by conglomerates, which are fundamentally financial and not production units (Magdoff and Sweezy, 1972, pp. 113–48), there is absolutely no room for the enlightened reformism advocated by Keynes. The financier cannot be separated from the industrialist because these terms do not define individuals but socioeconomic categories which today find their point of unity in the monopolistic conglomerate. Thus, while the *MR* position retains Keynes's analysis on the link between effective demand and investment, as well as the view that a monetary economy which enhances income out of capital and wealth is in the long run incapable of avoiding misery among plenty, the same position sees the roots of the contradictions of modern capitalism in the impact of monopolistic formations on the accumulation of capital.

From what has been said above, it emerges that the contributions of Baran, Sweezy, and Magdoff take up the issues raised by Marxist thinkers at the turn of the century. A comparison between the *MR* group and this debate is therefore necessary in order to show the analytical differences between accumulation in a monopolistic economy and in a competitive economy, such as studied by Marx.

2. Classical Marxism and the MR Group

The Marxist debate of the turn of the century focused on questions concerning the long-run development or breakdown of the capitalist system and the impact of the rise of trusts and cartels.[3] In both cases Marx's schemes of reproduction were used in their macroeconomic dimension, that is, as an analytical framework for hypotheses about the actual tendencies of capitalistic accumulation. The breakdown controversy has, in my opinion, only historical value because of its deterministic character. More specifically, the attempt to show on the basis of Marx's schemes that the system can be subject to steady accumulation or to economic collapse anticipates by more than 50 years the discussion about the instability or stability of growth models. The difference lies in the fact that in the Marxian debate, the object was the actual process of accumulation, whereas in growth models the object is purely represented by the properties of the models. As Kalecki once remarked, a curious division of labor has taken place in the west: on one hand, the government was trusted to balance demand and capacity in the short run, while on the other, economists would concentrate on steady-growth theory, in which the problem of effective demand and the formation of long-run bottlenecks were assumed away (Kalecki, 1970). The debate over the question of breakdown versus growth remained, however, on deterministic grounds because many participants tried to infer conclusions about the actual tendencies of accumulation using numerical extrapolations of Marx's schemes of expanded reproduction. By contrast a nondeterministic approach was taken by Lenin, Rosa Luxemburg, and also to some extent by Rudolf Hilferding. These thinkers did not try to interpret the possible tendencies of the capitalist system by mechanical manipulations of the reproduction schemes. Instead, they attempted to identify the historical configurations to which capitalistic accumulation might lead. The works of Baran, Sweezy, and Magdoff have to be related especially to this second group of Marxists.

For the purpose of our paper the analysis will be confined to Hilferding and Luxemburg. In his book, *Das Finanzkapital* (1910), Hilferding saw the source of crises in the disproportionalities arising between different branches of production and not in the emergence of general overproduction. Basing his analysis very much on the German phenomenon of the mixed banks, banks which acted not only as lending institutions but also as managers and controllers of industrial activities, Hilferding viewed economic activity as governed by cartels. The creation of cartels he argued, had a twofold effect on the dynamics of capitalism: on one hand it sharpened economic conflicts, while at the same time it led to a regulation of production.

The formation of cartels in different countries would produce a struggle within each country leading towards the consolidation of one general cartel. Social tensions and class conflicts would, in this view, arise from the economic struggle between different cartels. Hilferding also described in great detail how competition between different cartels could lead to a global military confrontation among capitalist countries. The possibility of a socialist revolution was seen by Hilferding to exist objectively in the class conflicts generated by the economic and eventually military wars caused by cartelization. Although cartels during their formative phase give rise to acute class conflicts, Hilferding thought that a fully cartelized economy would be more stable than a competitive one, a position shared also by Schumpeter (1928). In Hilferding's work there are many interesting observations which foreshadow much of the themes developed by non-Marxist economists after World War II. In particular he pointed out that the cartel's ability to regulate production makes the effects of a crisis to be felt especially by the independent competitive producers, thereby furthering the concentration of capital. A similar argument was put forward by John Kenneth Galbraith some 47 years later (Galbraith, 1957). Moreover, the concentration of banks which accompanies cartelization is bound to lead to a growing endogenization of money. Concentration of banks and their integration with industrial capital would eliminate, according to Hilferding, the need for commercial credit in favor of bank credit. The process of credit creation would be entirely under the control of banks. Gold, he argued, would be used only for international transactions. The endogenous creation of means of payments would therefore enable the regulation of credit itself, making financial crises more unlikely. While Hilferding considered the process towards full cartelization to be fraught with titanic clashes between cartels and thus unleashing formidable class conflicts, the theoretical thrust of his argument is that cartelization brings about a regulation of production and credit. During the years of the Weimar republic, Hilferding, who was to be killed by the Nazis, pushed this theoretical position to its extreme limit, virtually negating the possibility of crises (Hilferding, 1924).[4]

Hilferding's and Schumpeter's misconceptions about the alleged regulated stability of Trustified Capitalism lie in the fact that both looked at the concentration of capital through the prism of absolute monopoly while neglecting oligopolies altogether. In this way they waste the important point that in the advanced stage of capitalistic development, money is endogenously created. In fact the connection between endogenous money and the development of modern capitalism should be seen as an expression of the capitalist system becoming increasingly demand-determined and not as an expression of its self-regulating power. No such misconceptions arise in Baran, Magdoff, and Sweezy because their basic unit, the large corporation, is of an oligopolistic kind; this enables them to tie monopoly capital to the issue of the realization of the surplus discussed by Luxemburg (1968). The Baran-Sweezy book, *Monopoly Capital* (1970), sketches out the working of oligopolistic firms in a way which is by and large consistent with the more detailed analysis of Sylos-Labini's *Oligopoly and Technical Progress* (1969). I will start from what I think are the main points made in the second book.

The profit margins obtained in oligopolistic industries result from a pricing process in which the size of the market plays a far more important role than the elasticity of demand. The main reason for this is that oligopolies arise out of technological discontinuities and indivisibilities in production. These indivisibilities prevent oligopolistic firms from conquering the entire space of the competitive units. It follows, then, that oligopolies are not really interested in absolute monopolization, and this means that the elasticity of demand is not relevant, either. Oligopolies face, so to speak, a finite demand in a dynamic sense; structural discontinuities do not allow for the expansion of investment unless the market has grown sufficiently to justify the construction of new plants of a technologically determined size. We can see that the importance of oligopoly theory for a Marxist understanding of modern capitalism is deeper than many Marxists think. It outlines the structural outcomes of the process envisaged by Marx when he spoke of the rise of joint stock companies.[5] But the consolidation of oligopolistic formations changes the dynamics of accumulation itself. Perhaps the line of inquiry should no longer center on the issue of growth and crisis, but rather on stagnation, decline, and the possible limits of counteracting tendencies not just in the economic but also in the institutional sphere.

Oligopoly theory, especially the Sylos-Labini version of it, connects the forces of stagnation with the discontinuities of large-scale production. By discontinuity it is meant here that only firms of a certain size can install the fixed capital embodying production techniques necessary to obtain scale economies. Concentration creates the conditions for large firms to arise, and a structural discontinuity emerges because smaller firms are not in a position to undertake the required capital investment. Fixed capital appears therefore as a strategic factor in a concentrated economy, a control variable which determines also the nature of technical change. The theory also postulates that in the absence of an increase in effective demand greater than the increase in the total costs which would be brought about by the given size of new fixed capital, oligopolistic firms will tend to introduce innovations aimed at lowering variable costs, especially labor costs. The labor-saving bias of innovations is also linked to the role of fixed capital and unused capacity as a barrier to entry and as a weapon of deterrence against other oligopolists (Spence, 1977). Although wage increases following a rise in productivity will counterbalance the decline in employment as far as the demand for consumption goods is concerned, the economy will still move towards stagnation and decline, albeit at a lower speed. For if unemployment rises over time, the bargaining power of workers is likely to decline; wages will no longer move apace with productivity which, under oligopoly, means that profit margins will rise. At this point Steindl's link between higher profit margins and lower accumulation rates caused by, and leading to, a lower degree of capacity utilization comes into being and stagnation cum decline sets in.[6]

The observations about oligopolies and innovations made so far help eliminate some ambiguities contained in *Monopoly Capital* (Baran and Sweezy, 1970). In order to show that the oligopolistic corporation generates a weaker inducement to introduce innovations, thereby reducing the scope of investment opportunities, Baran and Sweezy refer to a point made by Joan Robinson that for innovations to occur under noncompetitive conditions, the rate of interest must be very low indeed (Robinson, 1956, p. 407). The problem is that in Joan Robinson's framework, and in particular in her *Accumulation of Capital* (1956), there is virtually no room for an analysis of the relation between concentrated oligopoly and production indivisibilities. By contrast, Sylos-Labini, following an argument put forward by Oskar Lange (Lange, 1944) shows that innovations also take place under oligopolistic conditions, but are likely to be of a labor-saving kind, thus accentuating rather than mitigating the tendency towards stagnation. Under these circumstances, the role of the rate of interest is of secondary importance and in fact becomes problematical altogether.

Baran observed that under mature capitalism the task faced by managers and policymakers "would not be slow adjustments to small changes—the main prerequisite for the applicability of the rules derived from static analysis—but choice among few technological alternatives involving large indivisibilities and 'fixed coefficients.'" (Baran, 1969, p. 147). This view, in an oligopolistic context, means that investment will be made only if the expansion of demand is large enough to enable the firm to overcome the increase in total costs connected with the indivisibilities cited. Hence if in a normal situation the rate of interest is reduced to very low levels, as Joan Robinson maintains, it will not change the labor-saving character of innovations. On the contrary, it should enhance that character. The role of the rate of interest in relation to investment becomes even more ambiguous if one considers two additional factors which are specific to the oligopolistic stage of capitalism: 1.) self-financing in the oligopolistic firms and reliance on bank loans in the competitive ones; and 2.) the form of allocation of profits.

The rate of interest, and therefore the policy of the central bank, primarily affects the borrowing of small firms. By contrast, the larger self-financing capabilities of big corporations create the structural conditions for capital markets to become imperfect. The potential ability to self-finance can be used to obtain loans on a preferential basis so as to maintain the desired degree of liquidity, thereby reducing the impact of what Kalecki called the principle of increasing risk (Kalecki, 1937).[7] From the viewpoint of the social economy, the investment and borrowing activities of the corporate sector have to be judged in relation to whether they expand employment or not. It is here that link between oligopolies and indivisibilites comes back in full force. If demand does not expand by the required amount, oligopolies can use their undistributed profits so as to 1.) invest in the stagnationist sense described above, 2.) become net lenders, 3.) acquire assets in the stock and bond markets. All these activities can be beneficial and necessary from the vantage point of the corporation, but they are not where the social economy is concerned.

The contradiction between declining real investment opportunities and expanding of financial investments has been one of the main arguments put forward by the *MR* group in recent years (*MR*, 1982, 1983). The weakness of investment activity is analysed in terms consistent with the stagnationist approach of oligopoly theory. But the argument about the growth of the financial sector is tied to the relationship between stagnation, inflation, and indebtedness. This raises a number of analytical problems, although the problems do not invalidate the way in which Magdoff and Sweezy present the issue. The point is that from the connection between oligopoly and stagnation, it is possible to derive a preference for financial over real investment.[8] It is also possible to derive a relation between oligopoly and the rise of the inflationary floor, and derive it mainly via the nonsymmetrical working of prices—raw material and food prices, as well as those of the competitive firms, tend to rise when demand increases, but oligopolies' prices do not fall when demand declines. It is, however, extremely difficult to build a consistent framework showing the interaction of these three phenomena. A partial indication of the possible transition to a state of indebtedness comes from Steindl's analysis of rentier savings generated within the corporate structure. This will be discussed in the fourth section.

In the context of the argument presented here, the main achievement of the works by Baran, Sweezy, and Magdoff must be seen in their having carried the Marxist themes of the long-run tendencies of capitalistic accumulation into the contemporary setting of oligopolistic capitalism. The causal relations between the productive and financial aspects of the system have yet to be worked out, which means that it is necessary to grasp the differentia specifica of accumulation under oligopolistic conditions vis-à-vis accumulation under competitive capitalism.

3. Competition, Monopoly Capital, and Structural Maturity

In two remarkable essays on monopoly and competition from a Marxist perspective, Sweezy (1972; 1981) made the following points: 1.) with monopoly capital the notion of a general rate of profit loses its significance—a hierarchy of profit rates sets in instead; and 2.) the extraction of surplus value is common to both competitive and monopolistic capitalism, although with the latter the form of realization of surplus value changes in a substantial way—on one hand, monopolistic corporations must take care of not spoiling the market; on the other hand, the larger volume of profits allow them a more rapid expansion via direct investment and easier financing.[9] The main contradiction becomes that of the increased ability to expand versus the more constrained scope for actual expansion (Sweezy, 1972; Levine, 1975).

Two important observations follow from the above. First, the problem of effective demand is far more significant under oligopolistic conditions than under competition. This does not mean that the realization of the surplus produced is impeded by underconsumption. The *MR* group, and Sweezy in particular, view the consolidation of monopolistic capitalism in a context of structural maturity, i.e., in a situation where the productive capacity of the capital goods sector is such that the investment priority should no longer be directed toward the formation of the capital goods industry (Sweezy, 1968b). This means also that the employment capacity (at near-full utilization) of existing capital stock and of related services suffices more or less to absorb the bulk, if not all, of the labor force (Kalecki, 1976). In the terminology used by Kaldor, we could say that structural maturity defines a situation in which labor and not capital is the potentially scarce factor, whereas in terms of Keynes's argument outlined in Chapter 16 of the *General Theory*, we would say that abundance of capital goods (which, when achieved, implies little or no income out of capital and wealth) is within a reasonable reach. Hence the basic disease of monopoly capital lies not in crude underconsumption but in a situation where "at anything approaching full employment the surplus accruing to the propertied classes is far more than they can profitably invest." (Magdoff and Sweezy, 1981, p. 148). The key expression here is "anything approaching full employment," which means that full capacity output roughly coincides with full employment.

Second, crises no longer perform the role of solving the contradictions of capitalistic accumulation, because their function for restoring the rate of profit and the rate of accumulation is greatly weakened; this is why stagnation acquires significance. To understand this point we must discuss the question of unused capacity, since it is via the degree of utilization of equipment that the impact of monopoly capital on accumulation and on the role of unemployment (or the reserve army) shows itself most clearly.

In the works of Kalecki and Steindl, unused capacity is the norm under oligopoly. But idle plant and equipment appeared also during the competitive phase of capitalism, especially during crises. By competitive phase we do not refer to static perfect competition but to the Marxian and classical notion of competition which allows for the periodic formation of unemployed resources, labor in particular. The primary characteristic of Marxian competition is that there are no major barriers to entry and exit. Hence capital stock and investment do not perform any relevant function of protection of profit margins. A corollary of this notion is that capitalists cannot influence market prices which are instead determined by supply and demand, a view very strongly and correctly maintained by Marx (1968a) in his famous *Wages, Price, and Profits*. Because there are no barriers to entry, those capitalists who have adopted a superior method of production enjoy only temporary exceptional gains which must, however, be invested as much as possible precisely because market positions cannot be defended by any other means. In Marx's words, competition "compels him [the capitalist] to keep constantly extending his capital in order to preserve it, but preserve it he cannot except by means of progressive accumulation" (Marx, 1974, I, p. 555).

The appearance of unused capacity during the competitive phase of capitalism goes hand-in-hand with the drastic fall in prices which accompanies every downturn of the cycle; a completely opposite situation characterizes excess capacity under oligopoly. Indeed idle capital equipment and decline in prices signals bankruptcies and business failures. To avoid failure, capitalists try to sell as much as they can to meet financial obligations. Since they do not influence prices, they cannot administer supply either and are compelled to sell even at a loss; "these forced sales play a very significant role in the crisis" (Marx, 1968b, p. 503). This financial aspect of the crisis highlights its competitive character, which affects also the movements in interest rates (Sylos-Labini, 1983b). Producers, in order to stave off bankruptcies, sell goods against cash and also attempt to borrow money to pay debts. Hence: "The rate of interest reaches its peak during crises, where money is wanted at any cost to meet payments" (Marx, 1974, III, p. 361).[10]

Under Marxian competition, excess capacity does not have the same macroeconomic effect as under oligopoly; idle equipment in conjunction with a fall in prices implies exist from the most-affected industries, entry in the relatively less-affected ones, and with the generalization of the crisis, the destruction of capital. However, when barriers to entry and exit exist, the mechanism, as pointed out by Steindl, works differently; the undesired amount of unused capacity can be eliminated by not replacing part of the equipment which wears out—a type of adjustment which is bound to reflect itself on the demand of capital goods and thus on aggregate investment demand. We obtain therefore the following picture: investment under oligopoly is also made with the aim of strengthening entry barriers by deliberately building excess capacity; this however creates the conditions for an adjustment mechanism which, when undesired excess capacity emerges, negatively affects aggregate investment demand, thereby perpetuating unwanted spare capacity.[11]

Baran, in his *Political Economy of Growth* (1973), fully captured the novel dimension of investment as compared to competitive capitalism. He also noted that corporations' ability to control capital stock is an improvement which enters into conflict with the private form of investment, viewed in an oligopolistic economy as demand determined:

> "In terms of a rational husbandry of society's resources, the capital-preservation policy of the monopolistic firm may be frequently preferable to the excess investment and the destruction of capital that take place under competitive conditions. Yet, as is often the case under capitalism, such advance in rationality as is achieved is perverted into its opposite if the monopolistic capital-preservation policy contributes to a shrinkage of investment opportunities and leads to a reduction of output, income and employment" (Baran, 1973, p. 200, n. 67).

In *Monopoly Capital* (Baran and Sweezy, 1970), the same point is reiterated in a manner which implicitly raises the question of whether or not unemployment plays the same role as in Marx's analysis of the reserve army. This is a very important question because, for Marx, the reserve army of labor is functionally related to accumulation; it helps restore the rate of profit and the rate of growth via the reduction in wage rates caused by competition between workers.[12] Thus, if unemployment no longer plays that role, we should ask ourselves what happened to the forces of accumulation.

Let us quote from *Monopoly Capital*, "In the older theories—and here we include Marxian as well as classical and neoclassical economics—it was normally taken for granted that the economy was operating its plant and equipment at full capacity. . . . " (Baran and Sweezy, 1970, p. 145). The link between a full-capacity economy and unemployment is expressed as follows:

> "In the Marxian theory, unemployment (the 'industrial reserve army' of 'relative surplus population') was assumed to be normal and to play a key role in regulating the wage rate. In the absence of idle plant and equipment, however, the unemployed could not be put to work to produce additional surplus" (Baran and Sweezy, 1970, p. 145).

By contrast, under monopoly capital:

> "Here the normal condition is less than capacity production. The system simply does not generate enough 'effective demand' (to use the Keynesian term) to ensure full utilisation of either labour or productive facilities" (Baran and Sweezy, 1970, p. 146).

On the basis of our previous discussion, the Baran-Sweezy position can be summarized in the following terms: Under competitive capitalism it is impossible to hold onto excess capacity because the fall in prices will cause a stream of exits and economy-wide bankruptcies; unemployment will cause, in turn, a decline in wages, creating the conditions for a recovery in the rate of profit and accumulation.

Now, if this situation does not obtain in an oligopolistic economy then the relationship between the growth of output and the share of profit, and between the rate of profit and the share of profit must be different from that hypothesized in a Marx-Goodwin framework of competitive capitalism. Indeed the model put forward by Richard Goodwin captures the essence of Marx's notion of cyclical accumulation, since in this model the share and the rate of profit move in the same direction, and unemployment helps restoring the rate of accumulation (Goodwin, 1969). At this juncture, Kalecki's definition of the share of profit as expressing the degree of monopoly becomes very useful, because it is valid only if unused capacity exists. To put the matter succinctly, Kalecki's degree of monopoly reflects the distributional factors composed by entry barriers and the like. It represents, so to speak, the balance of forces of oligopolistic powers. Unused capacity becomes a structural connotation of the system. In this context the share of profit is negatively related to the degree of utilization of equipment, to the growth rate, and to the rate of profit. (See appendix for a formal derivation.) If the rate of capacity utilization were equal to unity, the above negative derivatives would turn out to be positive; that is, share of profit, rate of profit, and rate of growth would rise or fall together as in the Marxian full capacity economy. We have come now to what we believe to be the most important implication of the Kalecki-Steindl-Baran-Sweezy interpretations of contemporary capitalism.

If an increase in the degree of monopoly (share of profit) leads to a reduction in the rate of utilization and in the rate of growth then, ceteris paribus, unemployment will increase. The rise in unemployment, by weakening the labor organizations, may subsequently cause wages to grow less than productivity, which under oligopolistic conditions implies an increase in profit margins rather than a proportional fall in prices. The degree of monopoly will go up further, utilization rates and the growth of output will drop; unemployment will expand. Roughly similar results can be obtained even without postulating an initial increase in the degree of monopoly. Following a very intelligent paper by Del Monte (on which the appendix is based), we can assume that the actual degree of monopoly corresponds to a utilization rate generating a growth rate of output below that of the labor force and productivity (Del Monte, 1975). If wages grow along with productivity, the system keeps going on a steady state with a given degree of unused capacity. Unemployment, however, will expand. If unemployment has a negative effect on the dynamics of wages, we are back to the previous argument; the degree of monopoly and unused capacity will rise, and growth rates will fall. In all these cases the reserve army of labor moves more or less apace with reserve production capacity. Unemployment might regulate the wage rate and especially the wage productivity relation, only to make things worse.

It seems, therefore, that in an oligopolistic framework the relation between the reserve army of labor and accumulation is not as strong as in the Marxian case. Unemployment remains a product of capitalist relations; it stems from the stagnationist forces inherent in monopoly capitalism, but it loses any major objective function. Unemployment emerges basically as a social contradiction. Kalecki's view that under oligopolistic capitalism the role of trade unions is to push for a reduction in the mark-up in order to expand employment, therefore, is correct (Kalecki, 1971).[13]

Our thesis that present-day unemployment would not favor capital accumulation, even if it led to a fall in wages, is not unconnected with the other aspect of modern oligopolistic economies, namely, that of structural maturity.[14]

The Kaldorian concept of labor being the potentially scarce factor, a point which was introduced at the beginning of this section, is applicable to a historical context in which productive forces reached an advanced stage of development. In Marxian terms this means that the production of means of production, the main source of accumulation, can by far outpace the labor resources technically necessary to operate them.[15] Kaldor has aptly pointed out that labor-saving technical progress cannot be relied upon to ensure the right amount of labor supply:

> "In order to prevent the emergence of excess capacity in equipment, the new 'machines' must be *so much* more labour-saving that the aggregate amount of labour required to work the newly installed equipment per unit of time, should be no greater than the amount of labour simultaneously 'released' through the disappearance of that part of old equipment which is worn out and has to be scrapped. This depends not only on the rate of technical progress, but also on the level of investment activity; and the condition will be all the less likely to be fulfilled the greater the aggregate amount of new equipment produced per unit of time" (Kaldor, 1960, pp. 114–15).

Although Sweezy does not tie industrial maturity to the scarcity of labor, his argument becomes clearer when cast in Kaldorian terms (Sweezy, 1968b). His observation that, when the capital goods sector has been fully built-up, economic activity should shift from the accumulators to the consumers becomes stronger when the productive capacity of means of production could turn labor into a scarce factor. But the attainment of this macroeconomic goal is, in the Baran-Sweezy framework, impeded by monopoly capital. Large-scale economies and production indivisibilities are the source of the potential productive power of the capitalist economy. At the same time, they also provide the structural foundations of oligopolistic capitalism. If entry barriers and the related price leadership contributed to the breakdown of the competitive Marxism process of accumulation, they would all the more act against the shift that Sweezy rightly considered necessary. Such a change would run against the raison d'être of capitalism, which sees investment as propelling profits.

4. Summary and Conclusions

In Baran and Sweezy the demarcation line is not between monetary and nonmonetary economies, but between capitalist and noncapitalist economic formations. Capitalism produces for profits. This is the monetary essence of the system, which in contemporary conditions is an oligopolistic one.

In Marxian terms, the relationship between monopoly capital and unused capacity generates a situation whereby a tendency of the surplus value to rise is not incompatible with a fall in the surplus value realized. This is the same thing as saying that, because of the effects of gross profit margins on utilization, a shift from wages to profit becomes in fact a shift from wages to wasted unused capacity. If we take the above perspective into consideration, we see that *MR*'s editors interpret the financial transformations in post-World War II United States capitalism as new ways to absorb the surplus and, also, as finding means to realize profit through circulation, when the burden of unused capacity sets limits to the rate of accumulation and therefore to the link between investment and profits.

The last theme, i.e., realization through circulation, is a relatively recent one, stemming from the observation made in almost every economic editorial which appeared in *Monthly Review* in the last ten years, that the financial sector has witnessed an unprecedented expansion in spite of growing stagnation (*MR*, 1983b). On this basis the conceptual separation is not between the real and the monetary sides of the working of the economy but between the financial and the productive dimensions of capitalism. Indeed, while it is impossible to separate between real and monetary activities (with the exception of very crude forms of theorizing such as Monetarism), it is extremely valid to ask why and under what conditions financial activities can multiply and prosper amidst stagnation in output and investment.

Although the editors of *Monthly Review* do not give an analytical answer to the problem, they have the merit of raising a Marxian and Keynesian theme in a manner appropriate to contemporary issues. As mentioned in the first section of this paper, the possibility of holding savings in forms which are not conducive to the purchase of capital assets was regarded by Keynes as a major factor in the rise of liquid investment markets and in the volatility of investment itself. In chapter 16 of the *General Theory*, the argument is repeated in stronger terms—in a mature economy well-endowed with capital stock, the long-term stability of full employment can be achieved only if investment is carried out even at a near-zero marginal efficiency (or expected profitability) so as to make capital goods abundant and thereby eliminating capital income. From a structural point of view, this line of reasoning is consistent with Sweezy's observations about the necessity of shifting the emphasis of economic activity from accumulators to consumers. At the same time, the multiplication of financial instruments can be viewed as expressing forces pushing the economy in an opposite direction to the normative conditions analyzed by Keynes in chapter 16.

Now, if we interpret the creation of an even wider variety of financial instruments as an expansion of the alternative ways in which savings can be held (other than the purchase of capital goods), then we must conclude that Sweezy and Magdoff are on more solid ground than Keynes, since in their approach the phenomenon is connected with the corporate structure of monopolistic capitalism, such as holding companies and the like. The Marxian theme lies, of course, in the rehabilitation of the notion that there are productive and unproductive sectors in the economy. The novelty vis-à-vis Marx is to be found in the argument that the emergence of unproductive activities is a result of a particular stage of capitalist development, a stage in which unused capacity is a chronic phenomenon setting limits to realizing profits through production.

The renewed emphasis on the relations between production and finance as embodying conflicting elements specific to the advanced stage of capitalism, is at present at the conjectural stage only, although this does not diminish the validity of the approach. The most noticeable shortcoming lies, in my opinion, in the absence of a set of clear hypotheses about the connection between oligopolistic structures, financial expansion, and stagflation. Magdoff and Sweezy are certainly correct in pointing out that the dynamism of the financial sector has gathered momentum under stagnationist and inflationary conditions; but how are we to establish the causal relations? As a matter of fact, a theoretical interpretation of the rise of corporate finance has been developed by Steindl. He maintains that the consolidation of profit margins under oligopoly in the presence of a sizeable amount of income-inelastic savings (dividends and executives' salaries) would tend to hamper the accumulation of business capital. Joint stock finance becomes, therefore, the instrument by which finance can be obtained. Yet Steindl's analysis is entirely oriented toward the explanation of the factors weakening accumulation and engendering stagnation, and it does not link up with hypotheses about inflation. Since we believe that Magdoff's and Sweezy's decision to locate the phenomenon in the context of stagflation is of paramount importance, we suggest that the identification of consistent causal relations should become the subject of the theoretical research of those who appreciate the validity of the contribution of the *Monthly Review* group.

The writings of Baran, Sweezy, and Magdoff, integrated with the contribution of Kalecki, Steindl, and Sylos-Labini, represent the basic framework for an analysis of modern capitalism. Conceptualizing historical phenomena is never a fully self-contained process, and this is why gaps and shady areas are bound to arise. Yet this is preferable to axiomatic theorizing where the laboratory of economics, i.e., history, disappears altogether. Their approach has the invaluable merit of preventing the transformation of economic theory into a set of technocratic exercises.

In this paper we have elected to put the question of structural maturity at the center of attention because it constitutes the point of convergence between Keynes, Sweezy, and Kalecki. In this context the oligopolistic basis of monopolistic capitalism highlights the crucial difference between accumulation and the reserve army of Marxian competition and excess capacity and unemployment during the age of monopoly capital.

Notes

1. An attempt to introduce Keynes's view of the disappearance of the rentier capitalist in a Marxian-Kaleckian context is found in Halevi (1983).

2. Steindl also points out that in the boom of the 1920s accumulation actually declined in relation to pre-World War I years. It must be said, however, that the 1920s were a period of profit boom in the full sense of the word. Productivity increased far more than wages, and prices fell only slightly. The slowness in the formation of consumption demand, connected with a shift in income distribution in favor of profits, created favorable conditions for financial speculation. Schumpeter noted that in 1929 only one-fifth of total investment was for productive purposes while four-fifths went into financial activities. Sylos-Labini characterized the 1920s as a period

of excessive profits linked to rising oligopolies and weakened unions (Schumpeter 1939; Sylos-Labini, 1981).

3. A discussion of the issues can be found in Sweezy's famous book, *The Theory of Capitalist Development* (Sweezy, 1968a); an excellent collection of the original texts appeared in Italy (Colletti and Napoleoni, 1970).

4. The Great Depression vanquished both Hilferding's and Schumpeter's views. The latter then thought that competitive forces were at work more than he had expected. Now, while it was Marx's great achievement to show that cycles and crises are necessary phenomena of competitive accumulation, it does not follow that when accumulation gives way to monopolistic formations, the capitalist economy becomes free of crises. The basic motors of capitalism, i.e., the valorization of capital and the use of money capital to generate additional money capital, remain untouched. What changes therefore is the form of crises, as will be argued in the next section. From this perspective the Great Depression can be interpreted as the first comprehensive manifestation of a crisis under oligopolistic conditions. We have already mentioned a study by Sylos-Labini (1981), where it is shown that the conditions for a collapse of accumulation must be found in the growth of oligopolistic power in the 1920s. Another study by the same author recently translated in English analyses the qualitative differences between the Depression of the 1870s and that of the 1930s. It is shown that in the United States in the 1873–1879 period, industrial output fell by 5 percent as against a fall in prices of 33 percent. In the 1929–1932 Depression, industrial output collapsed by 48 percent, but industry's prices fell by 23 percent (Sylos-Labini, 1983a). These findings are in line with those of the National Resource Committee's study in 1939. There it emerged that the decline in output hovered between 55 percent and 84 percent in oligopolized industries, such as cement, steel, agricultural machinery, and autos. The corresponding decline in prices varied between 16 percent and 12 percent only. By contrast, in less concentrated sectors prices fell more sharply than output. The most interesting case is that of oil products, where the discovery of oil fields in Texas increased competition enormously; prices fell by 36 percent and output by 17 percent (National Resource Committee, 1939).

5. Marx's point about joint stock companies can be viewed as a financial prerequisite for the development of productive units of an oligopolistic kind. Without joint stock companies, capital accumulation would be limited, also in a technological sense, by the capital in possession of each unit.

6. One analytical advantage of looking at modern capitalism in terms of oligopoly theory is to be found in the fact that the possible increase in the propensity to save does not arise from any Keynesian psychological law. Indeed, what appears as an increase in that propensity is the result of objective oligopolistic forces. It is worth mentioning in this context Steindl's hypothesis about saving propensities. The tendency of profit margins to rise is compounded in Steindl by a new form of rentier savings, which are produced by the corporations themselves, i.e., savings out of managerial salaries and dividends, all of which are highly income inelastic.

7. In Kalecki, the principle of increasing risk is formulated in order to highlight the fact that the level of investment is determined by the different amounts in which capital is owned. In the 1937 paper, he assumed the marginal efficiency of capital and the rate of interest to be given and running parallel to each other. Investment is plotted on the abscissae; interest and risk are plotted on the ordinates. Without the risk factor, investment will be infinite, because the marginal efficiency curve never crosses the rate of interest. Moreover, risk generates an upward sloping curve which crosses the marginal efficiency curve at some point; this is an ex ante formulation and shows that investment is limited by the ownership of capital (Halevi, 1975).

8. As mentioned before, Schumpeter has pointed to the contradiction specified for the 1920s, and the same contradiction was reiterated in recent editorials in *Monthly Review*. During

the 1960s, European economists considered the rise in the values of industrials in the U.S. stock exchanges in the second half of the 1950s as a sign of health, compared to the very limited role of European stock exchanges in meeting the financial requirements of European firms. Yet, if it is considered that in the United States self-financing played a dominant role and that between 1954 and 1961 the U.S. economy displayed a very strong stagnation tendency, then the rise of the values of industrials totally out of proportion with the growth of GDP should convey an altogether different message—namely, that new capital for real investment was giving way, because of stagnation to purely financial investment. (Lamfalussy, 1968).

9. By relaxing the constraint on increasing risk.

10. Marx's concept of competition has been used as a description of nineteenth century's capitalism by Maurice Dobb. Also, Sylos-Labini viewed the importance of Marx's analysis as related to the actual competitive phase of capitalism (Dobb, 1973; Sylos-Labini, 1983b).

11. An excellent paper by Michael Spence has formally shown the nature of investment for the oligopolistic firm. Spence's results show that when investment is made with the purpose of creating barriers via excess capacity the firm is freed from limit pricing; that is, it does not have to get prices low enough to deter entry (Spence, 1977).

12. The best formalization is still that of Richard Goodwin. Capitalists accumulate as much as they can; there is no problem of effective demand. As the capitalists accumulate, unemployment dries up and wages rise up to a point where the share of profit and the rate of profit fall to a level in which the rate of accumulation cannot ensure the absorption of the natural increment of the labor force. Unemployment erodes existing wages, and the share as well as the rate of profit rise again. Goodwin's model is partly truthful to Marx's because it is based on the Harrod neutral technical progress, which was not the case in Marx. Yet it correctly represents the functional relation between the reserve army of labor and accumulation (Goodwin, 1969).

13. It is worth mentioning that in *Wages, Price and Profits* (1968), Marx opposed the view that wage increases would be met by an increase in prices, maintaining instead that they would affect the rate of accumulation by reducing the share and the rate of profit. Kalecki's well-known article, "Class Struggle and Distribution of National Income," is Marx's *Wages, Prices and Profits* under oligopolistic conditions—trade unions should struggle against oligopolistic profit margins in order to reduce the share of profit, which in turn will lead to an expansion of output and employment. See also appendix (Kalecki, 1971; Del Monte, 1975).

14. Two points need clarification here. First, will a fall in money wages, accompanied by a fall in prices, lead to a reduction in interest rates with a positive effect on investment, output, and employment? The sturdy theoretical realism of Kalecki provides us with the answer. For the above effect to happen, the fall in wages would have to be of a long-run nature and the supply of money should remain unchanged even in the face of a lower monetary volume of transaction. It is quite likely, however, that banking policy would adjust to the reduced amount of transactions (Kalecki, 1954). Second, oligopolistic industries exist also in nonmature economies. But here excess capacity does not explain the bulk of unemployment, which originates instead among the rural areas and urban paupers. Moreover, the very formation of modern oligopolistic industrial activities in underdeveloped nonsocialist economies depends on the mature economies, mostly as a result of their direct investment abroad (Merhav, 1969).

15. Marx's schemes of reproduction and modern non-neoclassical two-sector growth models provide an excellent illustration of how the capital goods sector governs accumulation. If αK_I is the output of capital goods at any given initial situation and if $\lambda = K_I/K$ is the proportion of total capital stock installed in the capital goods sector, then: $\alpha\lambda\ K = dK + \delta K$, where d is depreciation and δ is the percentage increase in capital stock. Hence $d\delta/d\lambda > 0$.

References

Baran, P. 1969. National Economic Planning. In: *The Longer View*, New York, Monthly Review Press.

Baran, P. 1973. *The Political Economy of Growth*. Harmondsworth, Penguin.

Baran, P. and Sweezy, P. 1970. *Monopoly Capital*. Harmondsworth, Penguin.

Colletti, L. and Napoleoni, C. 1970. *Il Futuro Del Capitalismo*. Bari, Italy, Laterza.

Del Monte, A. 1975. Grado Di Monopolio e Sviluppo Economico. *Rivista Internazionale di Scienze Sociali*, no. 3.

Dobb, M. H. 1973. *Studies in the Development of Capitalism*. London, Routledge and Kegan Paul.

Galbraith, J. K. 1957. Market Structure and Stabilization Policy. *Review of Economics and Statistics*, May.

Goodwin, R. 1969. A Growth Cycle. In: C. H. Feinstein, (ed.) *Socialism Capitalism and Economic Growth*. Cambridge, U.K., Cambridge University Press.

Hahn, F. 1980. Monetarism and Economic Theory. *Economica*, February.

Hahn, F. 1981. The Preposterous Claims of the Monetarists. *The Times*, London, April 28.

Halevi, J. 1975. Kalecki's Conception of the Economic Cycle and State Intervention. *Annals of Public and Co-operative Economy*, July/September.

Halevi, J. 1983. Employment and Planning. *Social Research*, Vol. 50, no. 2.

Hilferding, R. 1910. *Das Finanzkapital*. Wien, Wiener Volksbuchhandlung.

Hilferding, R. 1924. *Die Gesellschaft*. Wien.

Kaldor, N. 1960. Stability and Full Employment. In: *Essays on Economic Stability and Growth*, London, Duckworth.

Kalecki, M. 1937. The Principle of Increasing Risk. *Economica*, November.

Kalecki, M. 1954. *Theory of Economic Dynamics*. London, George Allen and Unwin.

Kalecki, M. 1970. Theory of Growth in Different Social Systems. *Scientia*, May/June.

Kalecki, M. 1971. Class Struggle and Distribution of National Income. In: *Selected Essays on the Dynamics of the Capitalist Economy*, Cambridge, U.K., Cambridge University Press.

Kalecki, M. 1976. *Essays on Developing Economics*. Hassocks, U.K., Harvester Press.

Keynes, J. M. 1936. *The General Theory of Employment, Interest and Money*. London, Macmillan.

Lamfalussy, A. 1968. *Les Marchès Financiers en Europe*. Paris, Presses Universitaire de France.

Lange, O. 1944. *Price Flexibility and Employment*. Bloomington, Indiana, Cowles Commission Monograph.

Levine, D. 1975. The Theory of Growth of the Capitalist Economy. *The Journal of Economic Development and Cultural Change*, October.

Luxemburg, R. 1968. *The Accumulation of Capital*. New York, Monthly Review Press.

Magdoff, H. and Sweezy, P. M. 1972. *The Dynamics of U.S. Capitalism*. New York, Monthly Review Press.

Magdoff, H. and Sweezy, P. M. 1977. *The End of Prosperity*. New York. Monthly Review Press.

Magdoff, H. and Sweezy, P. M. 1981. *The Deepening Crisis of American Capitalism*. New York, Monthly Review Press.

Marx, K. 1968a. *Theories of Surplus Value*, Part II. Moscow, Progress Publishers.

Marx, K. 1968b. *Wages, Price and Profit*. In: K. Marx and F. Engels, *Selected Works*. New York, International Publishers.

Marx, K. 1974. *Capital*, Vols. I, III. Moscow, Progress Publishers.

Merhav, M. 1969. *Technological Dependence, Monopoly and Growth*. Oxford, Pergamon Press.

Monthly Review. 1982, 1983. Editorials on various issues.

Monthly Review. 1983a. Listen Keynesians! January.

Monthly Review. 1983b. Production and Finance. May.

National Resource Committee. 1939. *The Structure of the American Economy*. Washington, DC.

Robinson, J. 1956. *The Accumulation of Capital*. London, Macmillan.

Schumpeter, J. 1928. The Instability of Capitalism. *The Economic Journal*, September.

Schumpeter, J. 1939. *Business Cycles*. New York, McGraw Hill.

Spence, M. 1977. Entry, Capacity Investment and Oligopolistic Pricing. *The Bell Journal of Economics*, Vol. 8, no. 2.

Steindl, J. 1976. *Maturity and Stagnation in American Capitalism*. New York, Monthly Review Press.

Sweezy, P. M. 1968a. *The Theory of Capitalist Development*. New York, Monthly Review Press.

Sweezy, P. M. 1968b. A Crucial Difference Between Capitalism and Socialism. In: D. Horowitz (ed.), *Marx and Modern Economics*, New York, Monthly Review Press.

Sweezy, P. M. 1972. On the Theory of Monopoly Capitalism. In: *Modern Capitalism and Other Essays*, New York, Monthly Review Press.

Sweezy, P. M. 1981. *Four Lectures on Marxism*. New York, Monthly Review Press.

Sylos-Labini, P. 1969. *Oligopoly and Technical Progress*. Cambridge, MA, Harvard University Press.

Sylos-Labini, P. 1981. On the Concept of the Optimum Rate of Profit. In: Los J. (ed.), *Studies in Economic Theory and Practice*, Amsterdam, North Holland.

Sylos-Labini, P. 1983a. *Some Aspects of Economic Development in an Advanced Capitalist Country*. Social Research, Vol. 50, no. 2.

Sylos-Labini, P. 1983b. The Problem of Economic Growth in Marx and Schumpeter. In: P. D. Groenewegen and J. Halevi, (eds.), *Italian Economics Past and Present*, Sydney, F. May Foundation of Italian Studies, University of Sydney.

Tobin, J. and Brainard, W. C. 1963. Financial Intermediaries and the Effectiveness of Monetary Controls. *American Economic Review*, May.

Appendix

Share of Profit Utilization Rate Growth and Profit Rate

The investment function in the Del Monte model yields steady state solutions for any given degree of utilization.

$$D = auv\,K + bK\,q\,\dot{u}\,v + cK\,\dot{x} + zK$$

Where: $\dot{u}$ is the change in the degree of utilization u, $\dot{x}$ is the change in the rate of change of output x, q is the share of profit reflecting the degree of monopoly. Finally, z is the net positive effect on investment of technical progress expressed as a proposition of capital stock. Hence uvK is actual output whereas vK is potential output, v is the output-capital coefficient. By the same token, $quvK$ represents total profits and quv the rate of profit.

The proportion of investment decisions over capital stock is:

$$J = auv + bq\dot{u}\,v + c\dot{x} + z \qquad (6.1)$$

The rate of growth of output will vary whenever J exceeds, or falls short of, the ratio of saving to capital stock (S/K). This ratio is nothing but the rate of change of capital stock, k. When $|J-k| > 0$ a Keynesian situation of dynamic disequilibrium arises—planned investment exceeds planned savings, pulling up the rate of growth of output:

$$\dot{x} = f(J-k), f > 0 \qquad (6.2)$$

Capacity utilization will increase as long as output grows faster than capital:

$$\dot{u} = u(x - k) \qquad (6.3)$$

The rate of capital accumulation k is in fact equal to the propensity to save out of profits × the share of profits × the rate of utilization × the output-capital ratio:

$$k = hquv;\ \text{where } h = \text{propensity to save out of profits.} \qquad (6.4)$$

Substituting equation 6.1 and equation 6.4 into equation 6.2 and solving for the utilization rate u when $\dot{u} = 0$ and $\dot{x} = 0$ (i.e., for a constant utilization rate and for a constant growth rate of output), we have:

$$u = \frac{-z}{v(a-hq)} \qquad (6.5)$$

from which

$$\frac{du}{dq} < 0 \tag{6.5a}$$

Substituting now the value of u as given by equation 6.5 into equation 6.4 and putting equation 6.4 into equation 6.3, it is possible to solve for x under the condition of $\dot{u} = 0$, we then obtain:

$$x = \frac{-zhq}{(a-hq)} \tag{6.6}$$

from which

$$\frac{dx}{dq} < 0 \tag{6.6a}$$

Finally, the rate of profit (P/K) can be written as:

$$r = quv \tag{6.7}$$

Putting equation 6.5 into equation 6.7 we get:

$$\frac{dr}{dq} < 0 \text{ for } u < 1 \tag{6.7a}$$

Whereas for $u = 1$ the derivative is positive

$$\frac{dr}{dq} = v > 0 \tag{6.7b}$$

It follows, therefore, that if the utilization rate is unity, the share of profit, the growth rate of output and the rate of profit will all be positively related.

In the above, the Harrodian equilibrium growth can be expressed as

$$g + m = \frac{hqz}{a - hq} \tag{6.8}$$

Where g = growth rate of labor productivity; m = growth rate of population.

Because of the impact of the share of profit q on the degree of capacity utilization, there is no built-in mechanism assuring the fulfillment of the above equilibrium relation (Del Monte, 1975).

7 WAGE FLEXIBILITY, SOCIAL WELFARE EXPENDITURES, AND MONETARY RESTRICTIVENESS

Juliet B. Schor

1. Introduction

In October 1979, the U.S. Federal Reserve initiated a program of severe monetary restraint. The federal funds rate soared 2.3 points, and the rates of growth of the major monetary aggregates fell dramatically. This policy was presumably caused by a variety of factors: inflation was at double-digit rates, unit labor costs were rising at an annual rate of 13 percent, and real unit labor costs were increasing rapidly as well. On the international side, the value of the dollar was steadily deteriorating, and the current account was strongly in deficit. Given these developments it is not surprising that the Federal Reserve chose this time to undertake a program of restraint. What is surprising, however, is that nearly four years later the economy was still in the recession, or by that time depression, which had been triggered by the Fed.[1]

Prior to the 1979 downturn, the average length of recession in the postwar United States was four quarters. This compares favorably with the

---

For helpful comments on an earlier draft, I am grateful to Samuel Bowles, Michele Naples, Thomas Michl, Thomas Weisskopf, David Kotz, Gerald Epstein, David Gordon, and Morton Owen Schapiro.

pre-World War II period, in which recessions were both deeper and longer. The widely held view is that the reduced duration of economic downturns in the postwar era was due in large part to counter-cyclical macroeconomic policy. The central bank, like the government policy-making apparatus as a whole, was committed to keeping recessions short, and they were largely successful in doing so. However, the 1979 downturn proved to be different. Citing the need to control inflation, the central bank was unwilling to initiate a program of monetary expansion, with the exception of a brief period in 1980. It was not until the fourth quarter of 1982, 15 quarters after the peak of 1979:1, that the economy reached a trough. Over the period, the unemployment rate climbed from a low of 5.7 to a high of 10.8.

What accounts for the willingness of both the Federal Reserve and the government to keep the economy depressed for so long? Why, after past successes in quickly bringing the economy out of recession, did policymakers pursue policies which prevented recovery?[2]

It is difficult if not impossible to provide definitive answers to questions about what motivates human behavior. However, a plausible explanation of this change in policymakers' behavior is that it was due to changes in the cyclical sensitivity of wages and prices. Typically, rates of growth of both wages and prices fall during business-cycle downturns. In fact, some observers believe that a major objective of policymakers in triggering or sustaining recessions is the reduction of wage and price growth (Boddy and Crotty, 1975; Bowles et al, 1983). However, the degree of wage and price decline precipitated by downturns has fallen over the postwar period. This trend began in the 1950s and has progressed steadily since then. By the 1973 recession, both wage and price growth accelerated, rather than decelerated, between the 1973 peak and the 1975 trough.[3]

The causes of this development are largely unexplored. One explanation is that this development is due to a dramatic increase in social-welfare spending, particularly of the income-replacing type. Social-welfare spending may have this effect because it provides workers with an alternative income source to private-sector wages during periods of unemployment. This may reduce competitive market pressures, thus mitigating any negative influences of unemployment on wages. A second explanation, operating along analogous lines, is the rise of multiple-earner families. In the pages which follow, these arguments are presented more fully.

A summary of the paper is as follows. First, there is a discussion of the theory and evidence on the pattern of wages and prices over the business cycle. Next, the decline in cyclical variability is documented. Third, the relationships between multiple earners, social-welfare spending, and wage inflation are investigated econometrically. Finally, there is a brief treatment of related policy questions.

2. Wages, Prices, and Recessions

The argument that the monetary authority and government periodically induce recessions in order to reduce firms' cost pressures suggests that recessions are functional for profit-making in capitalist economies.[4] This view is central to Marxian economic theory, although foreign to Keynesian and neoclassical economics. Keynesians, who have traditionally accepted the existence of an inflation-unemployment trade-off, believe that policy-makers can choose any particular tradeoff and remain there. No periodic increases in unemployment are inherently necessary to insure the stability of the system. The new classical macroeconomists, on the other hand, deny the existence of the Phillips curve tradeoff, arguing that the Keynesian causality between unemployment and inflation is reversed. If inflation and unemployment are correlated, it is because economic agents respond to wage and price changes by altering their supply of labor. Recession is not only not necessary—it can be avoided if government does not engage in improper monetary and fiscal policy and if agents' expectations adjust rapidly and accurately.

By contrast, Marxian analyses of capitalist economies stress the functional and necessary role of recessions in profitable capital accumulation. In chapter 25 of *Capital*, Marx argues that "slackened accumulation," or recession, is necessary:

> "Accumulation slackens as a result of the rise in the price of labour, because the stimulus of gain is blunted. The rate of accumulation lessens: but this means that the primary cause of that lessening itself vanishes. . . . The mechanism of the capitalist production process removes the very obstacles it temporarily creates" (Marx, 1976, p. 770)

Marx's argument ultimately rests on the assumption of a conflict of interest between workers and firms. In Marxian (and neo-Ricardian) theory, profit and wage rates are inversely related for any given technology (Sraffa, 1960; Morishima, 1973) A capitalist economy, operating with a particular set of input-output relations, produces a surplus product which is divided between workers and capitalists. The division of this surplus product is a critical basis for the conflict of interest between workers and capitalists. (A second, related basis is authority relations in the workplace.)

Marx's theory of the reserve army argues that the surplus product moves cyclically, as a consequence of movements in unemployment, which alters the relative strengths of capitalists and workers. Assuming that technical conditions are unchanged over the business cycle, the following developments are anticipated by reserve army theory. First, economic upturns result in low and/or declining unemployment. This leads workers to ask for and to bargain harder for wage increases. Furthermore, low and/or declining unemployment lowers the cost to workers of losing their jos and therefore results in changes in work intensity, workplace discipline, and a variety of other factors which influence measured productivity. On the demand side, firms are eager to meet high and expanding demand, so they are both willing and able to pay higher wages. To some extent it is atomistic, competitive market forces (supply and demand interactions) which lead to wage changes. However, these developments (higher wages, lowered measured productivity) are also the result of workers' enhanced ability to organize, increased willingness to go on strike, etc. This view of cyclical behavior can account for the end-of-expansion productivity slowdown and profit squeeze which have been noted by various observers (Boddy and Crotty, 1975; Weisskopf, 1979; Gordon, 1979; Naples, 1982; and Bowles et al, 1985).

Downturns presumably have opposite effects. High unemployment creates fear and insecurity in workers. They are less able to resist workplace authority, organize collectively, or force wage gains from their employers. The reduction in costs, or the growth of costs, eases supply-side pressures for firms. With the revival of demand, conditions for profitable accumulation have been restored.

Thus far, the discussion of reserve army theory has not been specific about whether it is money or real wages, or both, which have this cyclical pattern. The literature and evidence itself is ambiguous on this question. While all observers agree that money wages move procyclically, there is not consensus on the behavior of real wages. Kalecki (1943) and Rowthorn (1977) contend that firms can always raise prices to cover increased wage costs. However, Bodkin (1969), Boddy and Crotty (1975), Kahn (1980), and Schor (1985) have found evidence of procyclical movement of real wages. On the other hand, there is also very recent evidence that there is no cyclical pattern to real wages at all (Merrick, 1982; Geary and Kenan, 1982).

Given that real and money wages exhibit divergent patterns, an obvious question remains: Which matters? Do firms care only about real wages, or what is more likely, product wages? Or do money wages matter as well? While it is beyond the scope of this paper to provide a definitive answer to this question, I will offer some a priori arguments.

If money wages do matter, it is presumably because inflation itself matters. Why would inflation matter? There may be at least three reasons. First, price increases make exports less competitive and imports more competitive. If continual exchange-rate devaluations are not desirable (because financial institutions hold currency as assets, for example) or not possible (as they were not during the Bretton Woods period) then domestic inflation will hamper trade competitiveness. In cases of competitive world markets and open economies, this factor may be quite important. This appears to have been the case in numerous European countries over the last 20 to 30 years.

Second, financial institutions are not typically able to protect themselves from inflation and historically have attempted to ensure low rates of inflation. Third, nonfinancial firms find that long-range investment planning is made by difficult when inflation rates are high and variable. For at least these three reasons, firms may care about not only real but also money wages. Similarly, the functionality of recessions may apply to their effects on both real and money wages.

Given these arguments, I have chosen to concentrate exclusively on money wages in this paper for two reasons. First, the empirical treatments of the changing cyclical variability of wages which exist in the literature all pertain to money, rather than real wages, with the exception of my earlier work. Second, the behavior of real wages in the United States, unlike many European countries, is not easily explained in terms of reserve army theory. Therefore, a detailed treatment of the cyclical pattern of real wages would first be necessary, which is beyond the scope of this paper.

The foregoing account has stressed the movement of wages, productivity, and profits over the business cycle. It has presented the Marxian view that recessions are functional for successful accumulation. In a broader, more political-economic sense, the business cycle, or movements in the reserve army, are closely connected to the existence and reproduction of a proletarian, or wage-laboring class. Indeed, the existence of wage labor is both the condition for and result of the business cycle. Thus, the character of the business cycle is critical in terms of both long-run growth and accumulation and long-run class relations.

In classical Marxian theory the existence of a proletariat is the essence of capitalism. A proletarian is one who is compelled to work for wages and who does not own or control means of production or income-producing assets.[5] Neither does he or she have secure access to an adequate consumption bundle through kinship or citizenship relations, i.e., intrafamily income transfers or social-welfare expenditures. It is precisely the proletarian status of workers which makes unemployment effective in reducing wages, creating fear and insecurity, and enhancing workplace discipline. If workers were not proletarians, a drop in wage income would be cushioned by property income or income from alternative economic activity, such as self-employment. Thus, unemployment would not induce desperation or strong competitive market pressures, and recessions would presumably no longer function to restore profitability.

On the other hand, it is the recession which reproduces the proletariat qua proletariat. For it is periodic unemployment which prevents the proletariat from either gaining a steadily increasing share of the surplus product or saving its way into the property-owning class. In the first case, wage reductions in the downturn restore the profit share. In the second, periodic recessions deplete workers' savings. Thus, in the classical Marxian view, business cycles are important not only to facilitate growth and accumulation, but also to reproduce the proletarian status of workers and the capital-labor relation over the long run. These two phenomena are, of course, not distinct, but two sides of the same coin.

Classical Marxist theory as described above is most relevant for what we may call classical market economies, that is, economies in which economic relations are primarily mediated by markets, rather than by state institutions or kinship relations. The United States, among advanced capitalist countries, is clearly closer to being a classical market economy than most. On the other hand, the European social democracies have less market-mediated economies, and Marxian reserve army theory appears to be less relevant for them. This paper will be concerned with classical market economies, as it considers only the case of the United States.

3. Changes in the Cyclical Variability of Wages

Apart from recent changes in the cyclical pattern of wages, there is considerable evidence in support of the reserve army model, for both productivity and real and money wages. However, in recent years, there appears to have been a change in the typical pattern. In particular, what has been widely noted is a decreased downward sensitivity of money wages and prices to recessions. As early as 1970 this trend was noticed, for instance by Robert J. Gordon in his "Prices in 1970: The Horizontal Phillips Curve." In 1975, the Council of Economic Advisers expressed concern about the issue. They presented data showing "that there is more resistance to moderating cyclical forces after the downturn in recent cycles than in earlier ones." And five years later, in the tenth anniversary issue of the *Brookings Papers*, a similar view was adopted by both James Tobin (1980) and George Perry (1980). They argued that because the cyclical sensitivity of wages and prices appeared to have declined, the major effects of recession were now foregone output and additional unemployment. The 1983 *Annual Report of the Council of Economic Advisers* noted that wages are now more rigid. Systematic evidence also began to appear for the twentieth century United States (Cagan, 1975; Sachs, 1979a; Schultze, 1981), France (Boyer, 1979), and a group of nine Organization for Economic Cooperation and Development (OECD) countries (Schor, 1985).

In table 7–1 I have presented annual rates of growth of money wages and unit labor costs at business-cycle peaks and troughs for the postwar United States. The pattern of declining variability around peaks is quite striking in both cases. In the case of unit labor costs, the downward trend begins late in the period. However, for wages it is steady over the entire period. This suggests that the phenomenon is not primarily due to the supply shocks of the 1970s. While it is necessary to take into account other factors, particularly the upward trend in the core rate of inflation, these simple calculations are instructive.

The foregoing suggests some clear evidence indicating a decline in cyclical responsiveness on the downside of a business cycle. To what cause or causes can we attribute this development? To my knowledge, we do not yet have an

Table 7-1. Wage and Unit Labor Cost Decelerations Around Business-Cycle Peaks

Peak Year	*Change in Growth of Money Wages,[1] Peak-to-Trough Plus 2 Quarters*	*Change in Growth of Unit Labor Costs,[2] Peak-to-Trough Plus 2 Quarters*
1948	−3.6	−3.2
1953	−2.3	−2.2
1957	−0.8	−2.6
1960	−0.4	−3.2
1969	−0.1	−0.2
1973	2.2	2.5
1979[3]	1.0	0.5

1. Wages are hourly compensation adjusted for interindustry shifts and overtime in manufacturing, total private nonagricultural. Source: *Annual Report*, CEA, table B-38, 1983.

2. Unit labor costs are nonfarm business sector. Source: *Annual Report*, CEA, table B-41, 1983. Calculations are the change in the rate of change from peak to trough

3. This measure uses 1980 as a business-cycle trough, as the NBER has officially done.

answer which is informed by systematic econometric analysis. However, there are several views on the issue.

The most widely held view is that declining sensitivity is a result of multi-year collective bargaining agreements. In various theoretical models, long-term contracting results in decreased sensitivity (Taylor, 1979). This view has gained widespread acceptance with relatively little empirical evidence. I would argue that it is implausible, for at least three reasons. First, multi-year contracting began early in the period. While there is no comprehensive series on average contract duration, there are data for various years from the Bureau of Labor Statistics series on major collective bargaining agreements. For instance, the 1956 median length is 2.1 years, presumably double the length in 1948, at which time multi-year contracting was virtually non-existent. While the steady upward trend to a three-year median contract length from the 1950s to the early 1970s is consistent with the pace of decline in cyclical variability, the evidence for the next ten years is not. From 1972 onward, there was no appreciable increase in the average duration of contract, yet in this period cyclical variability appears to have declined substantially.

A second, related point is that the proportion of the labor force covered by contracts, that is, union members as a percentage of the labor force, has been falling since 1953 and now stands at only three-quarters of its former peak. This development should result in more, not less, cyclical variability, if unionized sectors show less wage flexibility, which they appear to do (Mitchell, 1980). A third reason for doubt is that this phenomenon is common to a large number of OECD countries, most of which do not have long-term contracting. Only the United States, Italy, and Canada have multi-year agreements.[6] For these reasons, it seems unlikely that multi-year contracting is primarily responsible for the decline in cyclical variability in the postwar period, although it may have been important in determining the degree of wage rigidity between the prewar and postwar periods. Unfortunately, because of a lack of readily accessible data, it is not possible to test the contracting hypothesis for the purposes of this paper.

The second explanation for decreased wage flexibility is the increase in the number of multiple-earner families. This argument takes the view that the appropriate unit for analyzing wage and income trends is not the individual, but the family. It is assumed that families pool their income.[7] A multiple-earner family can be thought of as partially deproletarianized, to the extent that one member's earnings are used to offset the losses associated with the unemployment of another. Presumably the large increase in women's labor force participation in the postwar period led to a rise in the number of multiple-earner families.

The third explanation for increasing downward rigidity of wages is the rise of social-welfare expenditures in the 1960s and 1970s. While this hypothesis has enjoyed widespread journalistic attention, it has not been systematically addressed, to my knowledge. Rather, existing treatments of the relation between social-welfare expenditures have focused on other effects. Neoclassicals have identified the disincentive effects on labor supply, personal savings, and job search. Keynesians have been concerned with demand effects, a perspective which has been shared by some Marxists.

While these approaches are disparate, they share a common feature in their lack of attention to the relation between social-welfare sending and the reproduction of the capital-labor relation. That is, they ignore the effects on the relative strengths of workers and firms, which may be the underlying cause of changes in wage rigidity. If the view of a capitalist economy represented by Marxian reserve army theory is correct, the failure to account for the effects on power relations is a serious omission.

This criticism of neoclassical and Keynesian approaches is a Marxist critique; nevertheless, traditional Marxist analyses are not immune from it. Orthodox Marxists view the impact of state expenditure, for either social or military purposes, as an unproductive drain on the economy (Yaffe, 1973; Shaikh, 1979). The logic of this argument is that workers' consumption is constituted by purely market-produced goods and services, that state expenditure constitutes a deduction from surplus value, and that it thereby reduces the accumulation potential of the economy. Interclass dynamics are ignored, for the most part.

Neo-Marxian treatments of social-welfare expenditures (Gough, 1975; O'Connor, 1973) incorporate social-welfare spending, or social wages,[8] into the value of labor power. Social wages are thereby considered to be indirectly productive and aid capital accumulation.[9] This view is a considerable advance over the orthodox one, in its recognition that there has been a substantial change in the form of provision of goods and services over the last 50 years. That change can be characterized as a shift from provision exclusively through wage income and intrafamily transfers to provision through social wages (state transfers) as well. However, Gough and O'Connor overemphasize the productive nature of the new structure in an excessively functionalist analysis. Like the earlier views represented, this one fails to adequately address the interclass dynamics engendered by the growth of social wages.

Other work in the neo-Marxist tradition does address those dynamics. In particular, Piven and Cloward (1971) have persuasively argued for the importance of social-welfare programs in the maintenance of low-wage labor and existing relations of power in the labor market. More recently, their analysis of the current attack on the welfare state (1981) takes the view that ultimately capitalists were no longer able to use welfare-state spending to control workers and keep wages low. Rather, rising benefit levels and loose eligibility criteria eventually gave workers an income cushion which enhanced their position vis-à-vis capitalists. Similarly, Bowles and Gintis (1982) present an analysis of the effects of social wages in the United States, which suggests that the growth of welfare-state spending resulted in a direct redistribution of income away from capital and towards labor.

The essence of the notion of a proletariat is its lack of independent access to the productive capacity of the economy and its inability, as a class, to accumulate capital and therefore cease to be a proletariat. In the reserve army theory presented earlier, proletarian status is both a condition of capital accumulation and its result. Social-welfare expenditures, or social wages, are important precisely because they constitute an independent form of access to consumption goods which obviates the need for access to productive capacity. More simply, if workers rely on the state for their incomes, they are less dependent on wage income and intrafamily transfers.

Social wages can influence the strength of labor relative to capital in a number of ways. Most directly, the unemployment benefit reduces the market pressures generated by unemployed workers. It also reduces the fear and insecurity employed workers experience when the unemployment rate is high or rising. Similarly, workers' access to state transfers while they are on strike can make workers more willing and able to engage in and sustain strikes. Both these factors increase workers' bargaining power with their employers. The result of this increased power may be a decrease in the cyclical variability of wages, particularly on the downside of a business cycle.

The argument that increased social-welfare spending for the unemployed reduces wage flexibility has been put forward by Bowles and Gintis (1982), Piven and Cloward (1971; 1981), and Schor (1985), as cited above. It has also gained adherents among more orthodox economists. For instance, the 1983 *Annual Report of the Council of Economic Advisers* noted:

> "A number of studies show that wages and prices are much more rigid now than prior to World War II, and that rigidity has increased within the post-War period. . . . The reasons for this change are not well understood. A side effect of the provision of a "safety net" program is that employees may become more resistant to wage reductions, leading to increases in wage and price rigidity. To the extent that the two-earner family is a form of private "safety net" against the financial losses of unemployment, the recent growth in the number of two-earner families may also have contributed to increasing wage rigidity in the United States over time" (p. 39).

Before proceeding to the econometric estimates of these hypotheses, it may be helpful to look at some simple evidence. Table 7–2 presents data on the relevant category of multiple-earner families.[10] There are only limited data available, however the husband unemployed category is the relevant one. These data reveal a strong, upward trend in the number of unemployed husbands who have other family members who are earning wage income, from 41 percent in 1960 to 53 percent in 1979. This evidence lends a priori plausibility to the view that the rise of multiple-earner families led to less wage flexibility.

The pattern of income-replacing social-welfare expenditures also lends a priori support to the hypothesis. The evidence suggests a steady and dramatic rise in income-replacing benefits, due to changes in benefit levels, increases in coverage, and the addition of new programs, for instance Medicaid and

Table 7-2.

Year	*Weekly Income Loss (as a percent of total standard of living)*	*Unemployed Husbands with Wife or Other Family Member Employed (percent)*
1960	0.69800	40.800
1961	0.68300	41.700
1962	0.67900	41.500
1963	0.65500	42.600
1964	0.65600	45.700
1965	0.66300	44.400
1966	0.65400	47.500
1967	0.63600	42.900
1968	0.62600	48.200
1969	0.61700	43.900
1970	0.61000	45.400
1971	0.59200	50.800
1972	0.59000	49.100
1973	0.59000	47.700
1974	0.58800	48.700
1975	0.57200	48.500
1976	0.55800	47.300
1977	0.55100	50.800
1978	0.55500	49.100
1979	0.55300	53.200

Sources: Weekly income loss is from Schor and Bowles (1983); Multiple-earner data are from BLS, *Handbook of Labor Statistics*, Bulletin 2070, and *Statistical Abstract*, 1983.

Food Stamps. Samuel Bowles and I have constructed a detailed measure along those lines, which we have termed the *cost of job loss*. The social-welfare component of this measure is the appropriate variable for the purposes of this paper.

The cost of job loss is a measure of the income loss that workers can expect to suffer if they lose their jobs. The expected income loss is the product of the expected duration of unemployment and the differential between the wage offered by the firm (after taxes) and the income-replacing social wages offered by the state. We have defined it as:

$$CJL = UD \times (W - SW)/(W + CW) \qquad (7.1)$$

where CJL is the cost of job loss, UD is the expected duration of unemployment for job losers, as a fraction of a year, W is weekly after-tax income from wages, SW is the weekly level of income-replacing social-welfare benefits, and CW is the weekly level of non-income-replacing social-welfare benefits. This formulation thus expresses the income-replacing benefits relative to both wage income and the total standard of living of workers. Clearly, above some subsistence level, it is income-replacing benefits relative to the customary standard of living which matters for workers' decisionmaking, rather than the absolute wage loss. The weekly level of income-replacing benefits, SW, has been constructed by calculating two possible benefit packages available to workers (an unemployment insurance package and an Aid to Families with Dependent Children package) and weighting them by the proportions of the labor force which are eligible for each. For an in-depth treatment of these issues, see Schor and Bowles (1983). The income loss associated with unemployment is the CJL without the unemployment duration, or the weekly income loss. It is given in table 7–2. These data reveal a steady and substantial decline in the income loss over the period.

The weekly income loss has been calculated for the average worker and includes the major income-replacing social-welfare programs in the United States. However, because comprehensive data are not available, it does not include a few sources of social-welfare expenditures, most importantly, Trade Adjustment Assistance (TAA) and Supplemental Unemployment Benefits (SUBs).[11] These exclusions are not likely to have much impact on the accuracy of the measure itself, because they do not affect large numbers of workers.[12] However, the workers who are covered by TAA or SUBs are generally in the unionized sector. If this sector is particularly important in wage determination, as has been argued, either because of pattern bargaining or spillover effects, then the cost of job loss measure may underestimate the impact of social-welfare spending on wages.

The data on SUB plans and TAA are not sufficiently comprehensive to be included in the econometric estimates which follow. However, we can deduce some information from them. The most important fact is that workers who are eligible for these programs receive substantially higher income replacement ratios than those which prevail in the economy as a whole. In the case of TAA, Neumann (1978) estimated that in 1976, a TAA-eligible worker had average yearly take-home pay of $7,756. Fifty-two weeks of TAA benefits, far below the 91 week maximum, amounted to $7,753, resulting in a 100 percent replacement rate.[13] The number of workers receiving these benefits is not readily available.

For SUB plans, the replacement rates vary widely. In the United Steelworkers of America, 80 percent of the wages of senior workers are replaced for two years. The United Auto Workers have a similarly high replacement rate. And Ford and General Motors now have a program for a Guaranteed Income Stream of $13,000 annually for some workers.[14] The BLS does not collect comprehensive data on the benefit levels of the plans, so average rates are not available. However, they have calculated that 51 percent of the workers in their sample have some form of SUB plan. While the extent to which our income loss measure overstates the loss cannot be known at this point, the direction of bias is clear. However, it is also true that the trends in TAA and SUB benefits have been very similar to those in the programs we have included, so that the probability and/or extent of bias in the econometric estimates is likely to be low.

4. Econometric Estimates of Declining Wage Variability

In this section I will present an econometric model of wage change which tests the hypotheses discussed above. The evidence supports the view that income-replacing social wages reduce the cyclical variability of wages, which suggests that standard wage models are inadequate and should be replaced by a social wage augmented model. On the other hand, the estimates do not provide support for the multiple-earner hypothesis.

In a standard wage equation, wage change depends on the unemployment rate and consumer prices. While there is disagreement over the theory underlying the price term (does it represent backward-looking or forward-looking behavior?) and its precise specification, almost everyone agrees that these are the two critical explanatory variables. The most common form for standard wage change equations, is:

$$w = b_0 + b_1 u + b_2 o + e \tag{7.2}$$

where w is the annual change in nominal wages, u is a labor market tightness variable, p is the annual change in consumer prices, with some lag structure, and u is a stochastic error term. Over the years, other variables have been included in the wage equation—productivity growth, profits, payroll taxes, wage and price control dummies, and supply-side shocks. None of these has gained steadfast acceptance, however, and they are therefore ommitted for convenience.

Equation 7.2 was estimated using ordinary least squares techniques for the years 1960–1979.[15] The dependent variable is the rate of change of hourly compensation, adjusted for interindustry shifts and overtime in manufacturing. The labor market variable is the ratio of actual to potential gross national product (GNP). This measure was chosen because unemployment rates appear to have become less reliable as indicators of labor-market pressure. The price variable is the annual change in the Consumer Price Index, entered with a one-year lag. Other specifications of the price variable were also tested, for instance, a three-year weighted average, and both one-year and two-year lags. The results reported below are robust with respect to the alternative specifications.

Table 7–3 presents these estimates, which lend considerable support to a conventional view of wage determination. Both variables are significant, and the overall specifications of the estimates are reasonable. However, the hypothesis put forward in this paper is that equation 7.2 is misspecified, due to its failure to include additional variables which may have reduced the coefficient estimate for the labor-market variable. Therefore, equation 7.2 has been reestimated including those variables, the proportion of unemployed husbands whose spouses or other family members are employed and the income loss measure. Both were introduced interactively with the GNP gap and independently. Entering them independently as well is both more correct econometrically and allows us to ascertain whether they exert any direct influence on wage growth. Alternative specifications, including only the interactive terms (not shown here), yielded very similar results. In addition, due to the relatively small number of observations and the possibility of multi-collinearity, the two hypotheses have also been tested in separate equations, as shown in table 7-3.

The estimates provide considerable support for the hypothesis that income-replacing social-welfare expenditures reduce cyclical variability. The interactive term is significant in both specifications (equation numbers 2 and 3, table 7-3). Using the estimates from equation 3, the value of the labor-market coefficient evaluated at the mean value of the income loss variable is 15.52, compared to a value of 25.70 in the model without the interactive term (equation 1, table 7-3). Thus, the inclusion of social wages appears to

Table 7-3. Wage Equations, United States, 1960–1979, Conventional and Social Wage Augmented

Equation	*CONST*	*GAP*	*YL*	*(GAP * YL)*	*P*	*FAM*	*(GAP * FAM)*	$\bar{R}^2$	*D.W.*	*S.E.*
1.	−22.912 (−3.51)	25.705 (3.93)			.839 (10.95)			.861	1.61	.699
2.	−360.230 (−1.37)	386.73 (1.46)	414.250 (1.79)	−445.391 (−1.93)	.539 (3.10)	2.042 (.68)	−2.120 (−.70)	.921	2.13	.529
3.	−196.560 (−2.13)	216.815 (2.32)	299.711 (2.05)	−326.566 (−2.20)	.534 (3.48)			.925	2.03	.516
4.	−6.518 (−.06)	5.652 (.05)			.754 (5.96)	−.289 (−.11)	.373 (.15)	.856	1.83	.713

Notes: The dependent variable is the rate of change of hourly compensation adjusted for interindustry shifts and overtime in manufacturing, total private nonagricultural economy. *GAP* is the ratio of actual to potential Gross National Product. *P* is the rate of change of the consumer price index, lagged one year. These data are from the *Annual Report* of the Council of Economic Advisers. *YL* is the weekly income loss as a percentage of the worker's standard of living, or $(W - SW)/(W + CW)$ as defined in the text. *FAM* is the proportion of unemployed husbands whose wives or other family members are employed. (*GAP* YL*) is *GAP* times *YL*; (*GAP* FAM*) is *GAP* times *FAM*. *CONST* is a constant term. *D.W.* is the Durbin-Watson statistic; *S.E.* is the standard error of the equation the figures in parentheses are t-statistics. All rates of change are calculated as changes in logs.

considerably alter the estimates. The income loss variable is also shown to have a direct (negative) influence on wage variability. It is significant and has the expected negative sign, once the full coefficient is accounted for. From equation 3, the full value of the coefficient on the income loss variable is −20.65, indicating a significant effect on wage growth. These estimates therefore imply that the decline in the workers' expected income loss over the period 1960–1979 contributed to both an outward shift of the wage-unemployment tradeoff and a reduction in its slope. In general, the social wage augmented model is superior to the conventional one. The $\bar{R}^2$ is higher, the Durbin-Watson is better, and the standard error is lower.

On the other hand, the multiple-earner hypothesis does not appear to be supported by the estimates in either specification. This finding is somewhat surprising; however, it may be due to offsetting tendencies occurring in the structure of the family, e.g., the increase in female-headed households, which have not been taken into account here. Or it may be that intrafamily dynamics are too complex to be correctly captured with a simple test of this kind.

The results indicate an interesting finding about the role of prices. That is, the inclusion of the social-welfare variable results in a substantial decline in the coefficient and significance level of the price term. This suggests that standard models may be underspecified, and that the price coefficient is biased upward as a result.

5. Implications for Policy

In the introduction to this paper, I suggested that a key to understanding policymakers' behavior over the last four years is changes in the flexibility of wages over the business cycle. I argued that short-run movements in output and unemployment now exert less determinate influence on wage and price inflation and that policymakers have therefore begun to rely on long-term deflation to reduce wage and price growth. Furthermore, it was suggested that increases in social-welfare expenditures may have been an important casual factor in this development. The evidence presented above supports that view.

From this vantage point, one can speculate about the monetary restrictiveness supported by the Reagan administration. It can be seen as an attempt to raise the duration of unemployment, in an attempt to increase the cost of job loss. Similarly, the attack on the welfare state may been viewed as a desire to reverse the steady decline in the income loss workers suffer if they are unemployed. This suggests that the attack on the welfare state is not primarily due to political or budgetary factors, as is often claimed, but rather is an attempt to increase competitive pressures in labor markets. This view is reinforced by an examination of the particular budget cuts which have occurred, namely cuts aimed primarily at the working poor.

Both aspects of the Reagan program generated substantial costs for workers, and probably the economy as a whole, if we consider the long-term effects on demand, investment, and productivity growth. These costs raise questions about the interests that are being served by the decisions of policymakers. These questions are beyond the scope of this paper, but deserve careful scrutiny.

Notes

1. The issue of whether or not monetary restraint can in fact cause a decline or slowdown in economic growth is no longer uncontroversial. The dominant, but not uncontested, view is that monetary restraint can have this effect. I will here assume that the dominant position is correct, as a thorough discussion of this question is beyond the scope of this paper.

2. The official National Bureau of Economic Research dating of this period identified a trough in 1980:3, a brief expansion with a peak in 1981:3, and a final trough in 1982:4. In retrospect, the NBER decision appears to have been a mistake, particularly in view of the fact that the annual unemployment rate rose steadily from 1979 to 1983.

3. Part of the 1973–1975 acceleration in wage and price growth may be acounted for by a unique lag structure in that episode, caused by the lifting of wage and price controls. Nevertheless, the overall postwar pattern remains clear.

4. This view relies on a Marxian theory of the state in which the state is presumed to act in the interests of the capitalist class. While sophisticated Marxian theories of the state do not presume a mechanical relationship between state activity and capitalist class interests, all Marxian theories do incorporate that view to some extent (Jessop, 1977).

5. The definition of a proletariat is an interesting matter, as Cohen's (1978) discussion makes clear. Cohen argues for a more complicated definition than simply a propertyless class. Central to his discussion is the distinction between the ability of individual proletarians to accumulate capital and thereby leave their class, and the ability of the class as a group to do so. The proletariat as a whole cannot, whereas individuals can.

6. Sachs (1979b) notes that contract length in the United Kingdom may have lengthened recently, although there are not contracts of fixed duration in that country.

7. This formulation does not imply anything about equality or exploitation in the division of household income.

8. The social wage is that part of the standard of living of the working class which is not provided on the basis of the sale of labor power or kinship relations, but rather accrues to workers on the basis of their citizenship, through the state or quasi-state institutions.

9. In my view, Gough and O'Connor incorrectly divide social-welfare expenditures into those which contribute to the value of labor power and those which are necessary to ensure the reproduction of the domination of capital. The latter they call social expenses and argue that they co-opt the working class. This is an arbitrary distinction, based on political preferences, which I do not believe can be sustained in a careful attempt to actually measure the social wage.

10. Data on multiple-earners are only available starting in 1959.

11. Supplemental Unemployment Benefits are not from the state and are therefore, strictly speaking, not social wages. Nevertheless, I have included a discussion of them because their effects are presumably very similar to social wage payments.

12. The BLS has estimated the number of workers on SUB plans in 1980 as 1.7 million. This includes only workers under contracts covering 1,000 or more workers, which is four-fifths of all workers under contracts.

13. Neumann's calculations exclude fringe benefits, work-related expenses, nonpecuniary rewards on the job, and the value of nonmarketed time.

14. These data are from Easterbrook (1983).

15. This period was chosen for two reasons. First, it is conventionally used. Second, multiple-earner data are not available until 1959 and social wage data are not reliable after 1979. (The government has ceased publication of a number of the data series used in the construction of the measure.)

References

Boddy, R. and J. Crotty. 1975. Class Conflict and Macropolicy: The Political Business Cycle. *Review of Radical Political Economics*, Spring.

Bodkin, R. 1969. Real Wages and Cyclical Variations in Employment. *Canadian Journal of Economics*, August.

Bowles, S. and H. Gintis. 1982. The Crisis of Liberal Democratic Capitalism: The Case of the United States. *Politics and Society*, Vol. 11, no. 1.

______. 1985. The Production Process in a Competitive Economy: Walrasian, Neo-Hobbesian and Marxian Models. *American Economic Review*, forthcoming.

Bowles, S., D. Gordon, and T. Weisskopf. 1983. *Beyond the Wasteland*. New York, Doubleday.

Boyer, R. 1979. Wage Formation in Historical Perspective: The French Experience. *Cambridge Journal of Economics*, June.

Bureau of Labor Statistics. 1980. *Characteristics of Major Collective Bargaining Agreements*. Bulletin no. 2095. Washington, DC, U.S. Government Printing Office.

Cagan, P. 1975. Changes in the Recession Behavior of Wholesale Prices in the 1970s and Post-World War II. *Explorations in Economic Research*, Vol. 2.

Cohen, G. 1978. *Karl Marx's Theory of History, A Defense*. Oxford, Oxford University Press.

Council of Economic Advisers. 1983. *Economic Report of the President and Annual Report of the Council of Economic Advisers*. Washington, U. S. Government Printing Office.

Easterbrook, G. 1983. Voting for Unemployment. *The Atlantic*, May.

Geary, P. and J. Kenan. 1982. The Employment-Real Wage Relationship: An International Study. *Journal of Political Economy*, August.

Gordon, R. 1970. Prices in 1970: The Horizontal Phillips Curve. *Brookings Papers on Economic Activity*, no. 2.

Gordon, R. 1979. The 'End of Expansion' Phenomenon in Short-Run Productivity Behavior. *Brookings Papers on Economic Activity*, no. 2.

Gough, I. 1975. State Expenditures in Advanced Capitalism. *New Left Review*, no. 92.

Jessop, B. 1977. Recent Theories of the Capitalist State. *Cambridge Journal of Economics*, December.

Kahn, L. 1980. Bargaining Power, Search Theory, and the Phillips Curve. *Cambridge Journal of Economics*, September.

Kalecki, M. 1943. Political Aspects of Full Employment. In: *Selected Essays on the Dynamics of the Capitalist Economy*, Cambridge, Cambridge University Press.

Marx, K. 1976. *Capital*, Volume 1. New York, Vintage.

Merrick, J. 1982. The Anticipated Real Interest Rate, Capital Utilization and the Cyclical Pattern of Real Wage Rates. Unpublished.

Mitchell, D. 1980. *Unions, Wages and Inflation*. Washington, DC, The Brookings Institution.

Morishima, M. 1973. *Marx's Economics*. Cambridge, Cambridge University Press.

Naples, M. 1982. Industrial Conflict and the Rate of Productivity Growth: The U.S. Experience, 1947–1977. Ph.D. dissertation, University of Massachusetts.

Neumann, G. 1978. The Labor Market Adjustments of Trade Displaced Workers: The Evidence from the Trade Adjustment Assistance Program. In: R. G. Ehrenberg (ed.), *Research In Labor Economics*, Vol. 2, Greenwich, CT, JAI Press.

O'Connor, J. 1973. *The Fiscal Crisis of the State*. New York, St. Martin's Press.

Perry, G. 1980. Inflation in Theory and Practice. *Brookings Papers on Economic Activity*, no. 1.

Piven, F. and R. Cloward. 1971. *Regulating the Poor: The Functions of Public Welfare*. New York, Vintage.

Piven, F. and R. Cloward. 1981. *The New Class War*. New York, Vintage.

Rowthorn, R. 1977. Conflict, Inflation and Money. *Cambridge Journal of Economics*, September.

Sachs, J. 1979a. The Changing Cyclical Behavior of Wages and Prices: 1890–1976. *American Economic Review*, March.

Sachs, J. 1979b. Wages, Profits and Macroeconomic Adjustment: A Comparative Study. *Brookings Papers on Economic Activity*, no. 2.

Schor, J. Changes in the Cyclical Pattern of Real Wages: Evidence from Nine Countries, 1955–1980. *Economic Journal*, forthcoming.

Schor, J. and S. Bowles. 1983. Conflict in the Employment Relation and Cost of Job Loss. Unpublished.

Shaikh, A. 1979. National Income Concepts and Value Categories. Unpublished.

Shultze, C. 1981. Some Macro Foundations for Micro Theory. *Brookings Papers on Economic Activity*, no. 2.

Sraffa, P. 1960. *Production of Commodities by Means of Commodities*. Cambridge, Cambridge University Press.

Taylor, J. 1979. Staggered Wage Setting in a Macro Model. *American Economic Review*, May.

Tobin, J. 1980. Stabilization Policy Ten Years After. *Brookings Papers on Economic Activity*, no. 1.

Weisskopf, T. 1979. Marxian Crisis Theory and the Rate of Profit in the Postwar U.S. Economy. *Cambridge Journal of Economics*, December.

Yaffe, D. 1973. The Marxian Theory of Crisis, Capital and the State. *Economy and Society*, May.

8 KEYNES AND LUCAS ON MONEY AND BUSINESS CYCLES

Marc Jarsulic

1. Introduction

In their response to the current generation of monetarists who have adopted the so-called rational expectations approach to macroeconomic analysis, many economists have ignored a major point. While they have reacted to the reasonableness of the rational expectations hypothesis, and to its implications for policy under conditions of perfect and imperfect market clearing, they have tended to ignore the characterization of business cycles that rational expectations Monetarism attempts to advance. In the hands of self-conscious Monetarists—especially Robert Lucas—the assumptions that the rational expectations hypothesis is correct and that markets are best characterized as being in equilibrium are used to convince us that capitalist economies fluctuate not because of endogenous forces at work in the system, nor in response to the time lags and institutional rigidities to which IS-LM Keynesians appeal, but to shocks exogenous to the operations of markets.

These shocks are said to come primarily from the behavior of monetary authorities and to induce economic actors to make mistakes about actual states of the economy. These mistakes generate cyclical behavior of aggregate variables. From this perspective also flows the idea that all business cycles are qualitatively alike, in the sense that the movements of aggregate variables follow essentially identical patterns relative to one another over the course of a cycle. While they may vary in duration and amplitude because of the magnitude of shocks, all cycles are explicable in terms of shocks and auto-correlations they induce.

Since the Lucas perspective is offered as an explicit alternative to that of Keynes, it seems useful to compare his account of business cycles to that offered by Keynes in the *General Theory*. It will be argued that while Keynes's analysis provides the basis for criticism of many of Lucas's ideas, there are some strong and perhaps surprising similarities in their positions. Like Lucas, Keynes seems to believe that all downturns arise from mistakes on the part of capitalists and are not explicable by endogenous economic factors. He also appears to endorse the view that all cycles are qualitatively alike. These would be only similarities between Keynes and Lucas if it were not for empirical research which shows that that business cycles are not alike, especially with respect to their effects on income distribution. At times downturns appear to restore the conditions for profitability, and at other times they fail to do so, which has far-reaching efforts for the political-economic structure. Hence it will also be argued that the Keynesian perspective provides an inadequate alternative to rational expectations Monetarism.

2. Rational Expectations Monetarism

Although doing so neglects some important contributors, the work of Robert Lucas, conveniently collected in *Studies in Business Cycle Theory* (1981), will be taken as representative of the main themes of rational expectations Monetarism. One of his themes is a critical one, namely that formulation of econometric models in which agents form expectations about the future without learning from past errors, must ignore the fact that market economies give them strong incentives not to be so lazy. Instead he suggests that the more appropriate hypothesis is that of rational expectations, which characterizes the objectively uncertain future as having some probability distribution known to everyone in the economy. Every individual then forecasts the future, given knowledge of the distribution of possible events and the information currently available, doing the best job possible—which is taken to mean estimating the conditional mean of the variable in question. That is, if Y_t is a random variable the distribution of which is known and *It* is the information available at time t, then the rational expectation of Y_{t+1} at time t is $Y_{t+1} = E(Y_{t+1} | I_t)$. This will vary from Y_{t+1} by a random error, i.e., because of unanticipated shocks. The errors $e_{t+1} = Y_{t+1} - E(Y_{t+1} | I_t)$ are assumed to be serially uncorrelated with zero mean. The critical import of this can be seen by considering a behavioral relationship. If current consumption were a function of expected disposable income (e.g., $C_t = bE(Y_{t+1} | I_t)$), and taxes had been in place for a long time, one might observe a relationship between consumption and disposable income of $C_t = bY_t$. However, if everyone learns that taxes will be reduced in the future, current consumption might rise above bY_t, since it is influenced by factors for which current income is only an imperfect proxy. Hence relationships estimated econometrically will be invalidated by behavioral changes resulting from economic agents learning about the environment.

Considered by itself, the hypothesis of rational expectations is just another candidate to explain how individuals act when the future is not known. But when it is combined with the idea that the world is correctly described by a system of Walrasian markets, which are always cleared, it appears to offer Monetarists a way to explain why monetary phenomena produce autocorrelated trends in investment, output, and interest rates, while never causing any involuntary unemployment. This position is developed in several papers by Lucas (1981, pp. 179–296). In a Walrasian world, where all agents are individuals making decisions about how much to produce, how much to buy, how much labor to supply, and how much capital to purchase, the important information for making decisions is knowledge of relative prices, now and in the future. Since future relative prices cannot be known with certainty, even agents with rational expectations can have difficulty in separating transitory and permanent changes in relative prices, and in separating changes in absolute price levels from changes in relative prices. In "Understanding Business Cycles" Lucas (1981) suggests that transient relative price increases should produce increased labor supply among those producing a good (because of the possibility of a net gain in discounted future leisure) and inventory decumulation; while a permanent increase in relative price will produce capital accumulation by those making the favored good. However, since it is difficult to discriminate between absolute and relative price movements, general increases in price levels will cause increases in investment and employment, and declines will do the opposite (Lucas, 1981, p. 230). Since confusion of absolute price increases with relative price increases has caused excess capital accumulation, agents will need to adjust their stocks of capital goods downward. This produces a downturn in investment and employment. (In the technical example of this process given in "An Equilibrium Model of the Business Cycle," the investment cycle is in fact generated by a derived accelerator-like mechanism (Lucas, 1981, p. 197).)

The source of the confusing movements in price levels is the exogenous, policy-controlled money stock. Insofar as changes in the money stock are correctly anticipated and there are no distributional effects associated with the changes, individuals with rational expectations will correctly translate their effects into changes in price levels, and not be misled. Since, however, policy has stochastic elements to it, money-stock changes will also appear to be inducing relative price changes and, hence, will induce the cyclical behavior already described. The justification for giving the money stock the role of determining price levels is vintage Monetarist: "For explaining secular movements in prices generally, secular movements in the quantity of money do extremely well. This is a fact as well established as any we know in aggregative economics . . . ." (Lucas, 1981, p. 232). Lucas, however, has answers to standard complaints against monetarists—that they cannot convincingly establish the ways in which changes is the money stock affect prices in the short run, nor show good short-run empirical regularities. The fact that Monetarists need to appeal to long and variable lags between money and prices is only a sign that the Lucasian model—which postulates difficulty in sorting transient from permanent and relative from absolute—is realistic. If lags were not long and variable, agents with rational expectations would be able to reduce the stochastic element in price movements and monetary changes would cause little disturbance (Lucas, 1981, p. 233)!

This part of the Lucasian position may be summed up as asserting that the proper characterization of an economy is one in which agents have rational expectations, markets are in equilibrium, and the auto-correlated movements of variables through time, which characterize capitalist economies, are the result of exogenous shocks. Changes in the stock of money, induced by imperfectly anticipated and analyzed policy, is the major source of these shocks. The shocks induce auto-correlated movements in economic aggregates because they induce confusion about the movement of relative prices, the source of information for agents in the economy. An implication of this position is that fluctuations must be, in some meaningful sense, alike. Amplitudes and durations of cycles may vary because of the size of shocks and the correlations between them, but the patterns and interrelations of aggregates should be the same across cycles. When one thinks about this for a minute, it seems a very large and problematic claim. Lucas himself recognizes that the Great Depression, at least, cannot easily be explained within his perspective. This is a point to which we shall return.

In "Methods and Problems in Business Cycle Theory," Lucas (1981, pp. 271–96) tries to explain why the economics profession was diverted from the conception of fluctuations as qualitatively identical cycles and why that vision is coming back. The villain in the piece is the Great Depression. It seemed qualitatively different from previous downturns and gave Keynesian theory—which allowed for a non-full employment account of aggregate economic activity—a hearing and respectability. This respectability was enhanced by the apparent success of econometric models in validating aspects of Keynesian macroeconomics and forecasting aggregate economic movements over time. He attributes the resurgence of the pre-Keynesian equilibrium view to developments in the real world—stagflation and a return to cyclical behavior of a less dramatic sort, which served respectively to discredit IS-LM Keynesianism and make the Great Depression seem less significant—and developments in economic theory and technique: the ability to model stochastic equilibrium and the development of the general equilibrium-contingent claims approach to uncertainty, which could be wedded to produce models such as his equilibrium model of cycles.

The policy prescriptions flowing from this framework will take no one by surprise. Since the economy will always move to an equilibrium, government intervention can introduce uncertainty by engaging in interventions which are not fully anticipated, but cannot prevent involuntary unemployment, since it is assumed not to exist. Hence rules, e.g., steady growth of *M1*, and tax and expenditure patterns that balance the budget on average, should constrain government behavior. Then the economic mechanism will fluctuate only because of noncontrollable shocks, such as changes in technology and taste.

If one were to accept the Lucas view, many standard positions would need to be discarded. The most obvious victim would be the IS-LM version of Keynes. Another, as Tobin (1980, pg. 40) notes, is pre-rational expectations Monetarism. Like IS-LM Keynesians, their accounts of business fluctuations depend on imperfections in price flexibility to account for the effect of changes in the money stock on real variables. (A good example of this version of Monetarism is Poole (1978).) Since this adds up to quite a lot of discarding, there has been no shortage of responses. In his spirited defense of the IS-LM Keynesian position, Tobin (1980) argues that without market clearing, rational expectations still leaves scope for policy control of capitalist economies, since government policy can increase demand for markets in excess supply. This position is also taken in Begg (1982, pp. 154–61). Hahn, in *Money and Inflation* (1983, pp. 49–70) makes a similar point, arguing that nowhere does Lucas make adjustment of relative prices to market-clearing equilibria endogenous to his models, and that rigid money wages, with their attendant implications, are a reasonable outcome of a plausible adjustment story.

As interesting as these responses may be, they are essentially squabbles within the neoclassical fraternity. The next task will be to see how Lucas' theory of business cycles compares to that of Keynes, who is viewed by many economists as offering something fundamentally different from neoclassicism.

3. Keynes and Business Cycles

A first step is to give an account of Keynes' theory of effective demand, which is grounded in the *General Theory* rather than the IS-LM framework. (Similar accounts may be found in Johnson (1978) and Jarsulic (1981).) In Chapter 3 of the *General Theory*, "The Principle of Effective Demand," Keynes defined the aggregate supply price of a given output as "the expectation of proceeds which will just make it worth the while of entrepenuers to give that employment" (Keynes, 1973, p. 25). Since Keynes was thinking in marginalist terms, the aggregate supply schedule was implicitly derived from marginal-cost curves. That is, for a firm which has labor as the only variable input, cost curves can be represented as in figure 8-1a. At the expected price level P_o, a profit maximizing firm is induced to produce Q_o. The aggregate supply price for Q_o is $P_o \times Q_o$. Since output is a function of employment, the aggregate supply price is $w[f(N_o)/f'(N_o)]$, where w is the money wage, $f(N)$ is the production function, and N is labor input. The aggregate supply price of this firm will change in proportion to changes

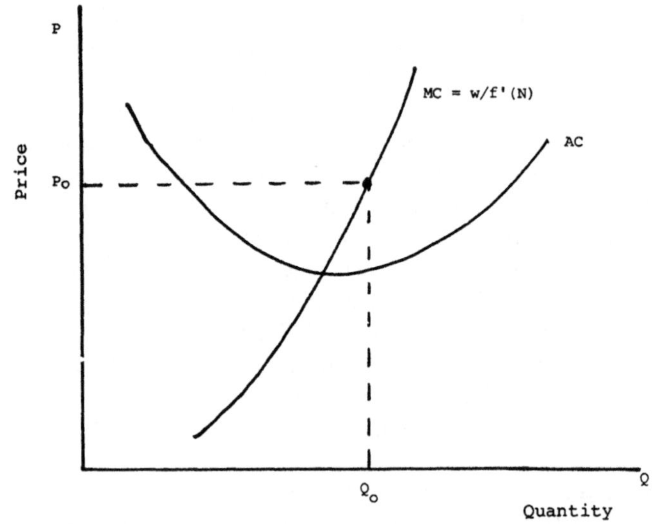

Figure 8-1a

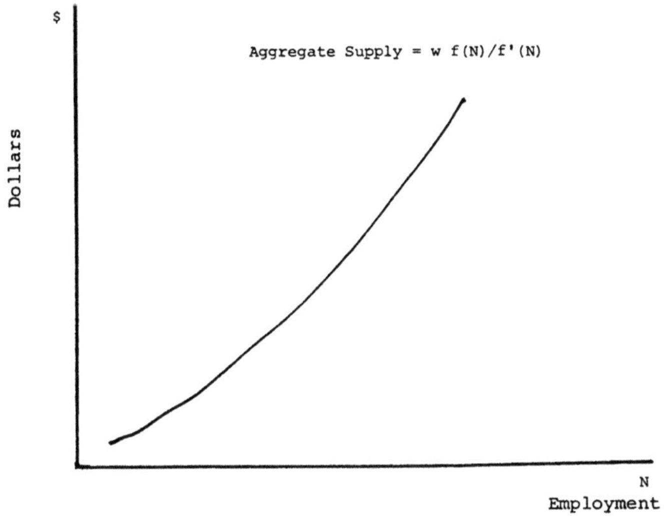

Figure 8-1b

in the money-wage rate. Taking this firm as representative of firms throughout the economy, the aggregate supply curve for the economy can be drawn as in figure 8-1b. Given a money wage, expected prices and total revenues must rise if output is to increase.

An aggregate demand schedule is derived from the division of demand into consumption and investment. If consumption is a fraction $(1 > c > 0)$ of income and the real level of investment demand (I) is given, the aggregate demand schedule will look like that shown in figure 8–2. The point of intersection of the two schedules is the point of effective demand. Here firms are maximizing profits, and supply is equal to demand in all goods markets.

With this apparatus, Keynes was prepared to call into question the marginalist analysis of output and employment. Suppose that real investment demand and the money-wage rate are given. Need the point of effective demand, and the amount of employment corresponding to it, determine employment at the full-employment level in the micro labor market sense? The somewhat startling answer is no. It seems perfectly possible to have a situation as depicted in figure 8–2, where aggregate supply equals aggregate demand, but labor supply exceeds labor demand at a real wage above the micro equilibrium level $(w/p)_e$.

There were, however, several large *ceteris paribus* assumptions which opened up the discussion of this possibility. Money wages were assumed

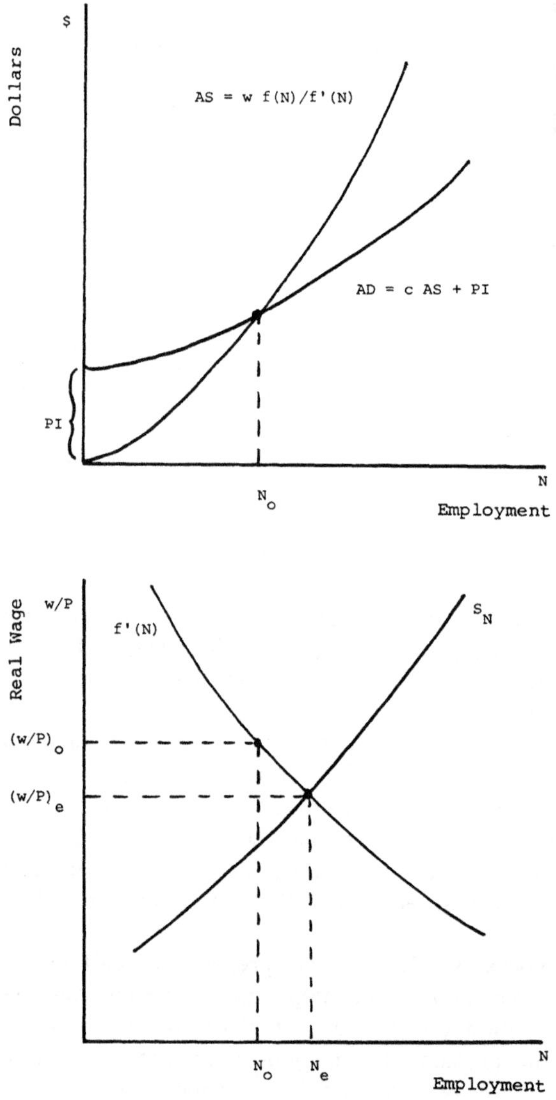

Figure 8-2

given, as was the level of real investment demand. The next important question is how relaxing these assumptions affects the critique of micro theory. If we still hold investment demand constant, an examination of figure 8–2 indicates that flexible money-wages would not restore full employment.

At first this might seem implausible. Should not a decline in money wages lower the real wage and, therefore, increase employment by profit maximizing firms? This would be true if the price level were constant. But Keynes has taken micro theory at its word, assuming price is equal to marginal cost. Since marginal cost is composed of the money-wage cost of labor, a fall in money wages reduces prices by the same proportion. Hence the real wage stays the same and so does employment. In terms of figure 8–2, a fall in w shifts the aggregate demand and supply functions proportionately, so their intersection is still an employment level N_o.

The conclusion from this is that unless there is something about the behavior of real investment demand—perhaps in conjunction with falling money wages—which automatically increases real investment during times of excess labor supply, there will be no automatic tendency to full employment. The analysis of investment which Keynes provided to complete this picture involves the marginal efficiency of capital. For Keynes the inducement to invest was the prospect of profit, not the current realization of profit. The marginal efficiency was defined as the rate of discount, which equated the expected returns from some investment project to its supply price (Keynes, 1973, pp. 135–36). As Robinson (1979, pp. 56–57) and Pasinetti (1974, pp. 36–37) have pointed out, this amounts to defining an expected rate of profit for a project. The expected rate of profit of possible projects would then be compared to the money rate of interest; where the expected rate of profit exceeded the rate of interest the project would be carried out.

In chapters 5 and 12 of the *General Theory*, Keynes discussed the formation of long-term expectations of profitability. He made clear that calculation of probabilities of future events is virtually impossible and that, instead, practical men are forced to operate with rules of thumb and out of ignorance. This makes investment decisions ultimately rest on "animal spirits" (Keynes, 1973, pp. 161–63). While rules of thumb and attention to current results make for steady expectations much of the time, this kind of uncertainty leaves estimates of profitability subject to large revisions from time to time.

With the importance of expectations brought to the fore, it is possible to argue that abandoning the assumption of a fixed level of real investment demand is still insufficient for full employment to be a necessary outcome of money wage and price flexibility. With a given rate of interest, an increase in the marginal efficiency of capital would be required to raise real investment demand. Declining money wages, caused by an excess supply of labor, need not bring this about. For while this would reduce the cost of investment goods, it might reasonably be expected that wages will continue to fall in the future, reducing money revenues. Hence a fall in money wages need not increase the profitability of any particular investment project; it might in fact reduce it. Thus even if the rate of interest falls with a falling price level, there is no necessity that aggregate demand and employment will increase.

It is easy to see that the *General Theory* develops several lines of criticism of the rational expectations version of Monetarism. The idea that capitalists can meaningfully be represented as knowing the objective probability distribution of future events seems difficult to accept in light of Keynes' discussion of long-term expectations. In addition, while Keynes' description of price formation is incomplete, his explicit connection of money wage and price levels seems to demonstrate that, with endogenous formation of relative prices, there is no *a priori* reason to believe that marginalist analysis can show why labor markets must clear. These aspects of Keynes' position are vigorously embraced by many who call themselves post-Keynesians (Davidson and Kregel, 1981; Weintraub, 1978, Ch. 2), and they seem to regard them as a sufficient basis for a theoretical alternative.

Although an appeal to uncertainty and shifting estimates of profitability might provide a plausible explanation why capitalist economies sometimes fluctuate around normal levels of capacity utilization, it is not at all obvious how it can be used to acount for serious, prolonged crises like the Great Depression or the current depression. If capitalists as a group made one estimate of profits in 1930, why did it take them a decade to make significantly different estimates? Keynes' explanation, in chapter 22 of the *General Theory*, is a mixture of psychological and objective factors. Downturns come when capitalists realize that the rate of profit necessary to sustain current levels of capital investment cannot be achieved and reduce their level of investment. Serious downturns begin with the recognition that large miscalculations have been made. Along with the decline in aggregate demand comes a decline in business confidence. Thus Keynes (1973, pp. 321–22) writes that " . . . it is an essential characteristic of the boom that investments which will in fact yield, say, 2 percent in conditions of full employment are made in the expectation of a yield of, say, 6 percent, and are valued accordingly. When the disillusion comes, this expectation is replaced by a contrary 'error of pessimism,' with the result that the investments, which would in fact yield 2 percent in conditions of full employment, are expected to yield less than nothing; and the resulting state of collapse of new investment then leads to a state of unemployment in which investments, which would have yielded 2 percent in conditions of full employment, in fact yield less than nothing." Recovery of confidence and investment demand comes about through the economic destruction of capital stock which restores the potential rate of profit (Keynes, 1973, pp. 317–19). He also seems to believe that low rates of profit are compatible with full-employment operation of capitalist economies if long-term interest rates could be lowered sufficiently, or if income could be redistributed to raise aggregate demand (Keynes, 1973, pp. 322–24).

Thus it might be said that Keynes, like Lucas, believes that business cycles are exogenously caused and qualitatively alike. His explanation of how they come about appeals to a different expectations mechanism, which allows mistakes to be generated by something other than the exogenous stock of money, and his approach is designed to show that, even with price flexibility, the labor market need not clear. However, in a significant respect these otherwise divergent theories are the same.

Of course it might be objected that the Keynesian approach admits of other interpretations that do not tie one to a belief in incorrect expectations as the source of qualitatively similar cycles. Yet the two major attempts to modify Keynes's theory of cycles have serious drawbacks. The multiplier-accelerator model, for example, offers an endogenous theory of the cycle, based on lags in response. However this model, as Pasinetti (1974, pp. 54–85) shows, is incapable of generating both growth and cycles. If growth is allowed for, cycles must originate in exogenous shocks. Moreover, cycles are qualitatively alike. A second approach, the financial instability hypothesis of Minsky, (1982, pp. 59–70), also offers an endogenous theory of cycles. Minsky argues that as capitalist economies begin to expand, firms feel increasingly comfortable with external finance. The exhilaration of economic expansion tempts them to carry increasingly large debts, and financial institutions go along with them. This financial overextension creates increasing financial instability, and when something goes wrong for an important institution or set of institutions, their inability to meet their financial commitments can trigger a financial crisis for the entire economy. This is a necessary and sufficient condition for a downturn. Thus, for Minsky, cycles are qualitatively alike. One difficulty for this approach is separating cause from effect. The empirical work of Pollin (1982) suggests that the increased dependence of firms on external finance as expansions continue can be accounted for by the declining flow of internal funds. This means that the appeal to psychological exhilaration may not be an adequate foundation for an account of cycles.

While this is by no means a complete survey of approaches to cycles inspired by Keynes, it does indicate that his theory places significant constraints on attempts to develop a theory of business cycles. Next we will try to indicate the existence of empirical work which implies that these conceptual constraints, also common to rational expectations Monetarism, are at variance with fact.

4. Recent Findings on Business Cycles

There is a growing body of empirical work, stimulated by the Marxist theoretical tradition, which offers a challenge to the idea that business cycles are all alike. The study by Gordon et al (1983), for example, is based on the Marxian idea that, normally, downturns perform a significant social function—the restoration of potential profitability through the reduction of labor's share in net product. In this sense downturns are normally reproductive of capitalist systems, since they restore the conditions necessary for capital accumulation. If downturns are unable to do this, and the profits necessary to stimulate accumulation are not there, one might reasonably expect a tendency to deeper downturns together with political and economic changes designed to restore profits. In fact Gordon et al (1983) find that for the period 1890–1981 in the United States, major crises—e.g., the severe downturns of 1929–1937 and 1973–1979—are preceded by nonreproductive downturns which failed to reduce labor's share in net product.

In *Segmented Work, Divided Workers*, Gordon et al (1982) offer a detailed account of the connections between the organization of the labor process, accumulation, and major economic downturns. There they argue that major crises are generated by failures in the institutional organization of the workplace and the labor market, which prevent the achievement of profitability and, therefore, capital accumulation. When this occurs it becomes necessary to reorganize the labor process—for example to transform the faltering drive system of the early twentieth century to the current bureaucratic, segmented labor-market system—and to create an institutional environment consistent with the new organization of work. This complex of institutions—financial, governmental, and labor market—is called a social structure of accumulation. They argue that duration of major downturns is determined by the time it takes to construct an adequate new social structure of accumulation. Whether or not one accepts their theoretical framework, the close connections they establish between institutional failures and major economic downturns casts serious doubts on economic models which treat all cycles as if they were identical.

Studies of the post-World War II U.S. economy make a case for regarding the aggregate demand problems of the 1970s and 1980s as somewhat different from earlier postwar downturns. In a careful study of the nonfinancial corporate sector, Weisskopf (1979) shows a definite downward trend in the rate of profit in the period after 1966. His analysis attributes this to a rising share of labor in net product, rather than to changes in capacity utilization or capital intensity. The theoretical explanation offered is the rising strength of labor relative to capital. In a similar vein, the paper by Schor (in this volume) points to a decreasing ability of cyclical pressure to reduce money wages over the same period. Within this context it is possible to maintain that the severity and duration of current problems arise from the unfavorable position in which business now finds itself, which makes the present situation qualitatively different from downturns in the 1940s and 1950s.

These studies also point to an endogenous explanation for major downturns: The relative strength of labor, manifest in the workplace and the political arena, arises in such a way that the share of profits in net income is reduced. This causes a decline in accumulation until the conditions for profitability can be restored. In this respect they offer a strong, though in many ways still evolving, alternative to the Monetarist and Keynesian theory of cycles.

5. Conclusion

It has been argued in the foregoing that while there are significant differences between the newest version of Monetarism and Keynes' theoretical perspective, there are some strong similarities with respect to their characterization of business cycles. Much recent empirical work by Marxist economists casts serious doubt on the these shared ideas. The recalcitrant facts were discovered because the Marxian theory said they should be there. This is a *prima facie* indication that the Keynesian theory of effective demand needs to be integrated with at least some of the elements of the Marxian theory of class and income distribution if a satisfactory account of cyclical behavior is to be developed.

References

Begg, D. K. H. 1982. *The Rational Expectations Revolution in Macroeconomics*. Baltimore, Maryland, The Johns Hopkins University Press.

Davidson, P. and J. Kregel. 1980. Keynes' Paradigm: A Theoretical Framework for Monetary Analysis. In: E. Nell (ed.), *Growth, Profits and Property*, New York, Cambridge University Press.

Gordon, D., R. Edwards, and M. Reich. 1982. *Segmented Work, Divided Workers*. New York, Cambridge University Press.

Gordon, D., T. Weisskopf, and S. Bowles. 1983. Long Swings and the Nonreproductive Cycle. *American Economic Review*, May.

Hahn, F. 1983. *Money and Inflation*. Cambridge, MA, The MIT Press.

Jarsulic, M. 1981. Unemployment in a Flexible Price Competitive Model. *Journal of Post-Keynesian Economics*, Fall.

Johnson, I. 1978. A Revised Perspective on Keynes' *General Theory*. *Journal of Economic Issues*, September.

Keynes, J. M. 1973. *The General Theory of Employment, Interest and Money*. New York, Macmillan.

Lucas, R. 1981. *Studies in Business Cycle Theory*. Cambridge, MA, The MIT Press.

Minsky, H. 1982. *Can "It" Happen Again*? Armonk, NY, M. E. Sharpe.

Pasinetti, L. 1974. *Growth and Income Distribution*. New York, Cambridge University Press.

Pollin, R. 1982. Corporate Financial Structures and the Crisis of U.S. Capitalism. Ph.D. dissertation, New School for Social Research.

Poole, W. 1978. *Money and the Economy: A Monetarist View*. Reading, MA, Addison-Wesley.

Robinson, J. 1979. *Contributions to Modern Economics*. Oxford, Basil Blackwell.

Tobin, J. 1980. *Asset Accumulation and Economic Activity*. Oxford, Basil Blackwell.

Weintraub, S. 1978. *Keynes, Keynesians and Monetarists*. Philadelphia, PA, University of Pennsylvania Press.

Weisskopf, T. 1979. Marxian Crisis Theory and the Rate of Profit in the Post-War U.S. Economy. *Cambridge Journal of Economics*, December.

Name Index

Subject Index

GPSR Compliance

The European Union's (EU) General Product Safety Regulation (GPSR) is a set of rules that requires consumer products to be safe and our obligations to ensure this.

If you have any concerns about our products, you can contact us on ProductSafety@springernature.com

In case Publisher is established outside the EU, the EU authorized representative is:

Springer Nature Customer Service Center GmbH
Europaplatz 3
69115 Heidelberg, Germany

Batch number: 10823959

Printed by Printforce, the Netherlands